# GARDEN PARTIES

PHOTOGRAPHS BY MICHAEL LUPPINO

CLARKSON POTTER / PUBLISHERS
NEW YORK

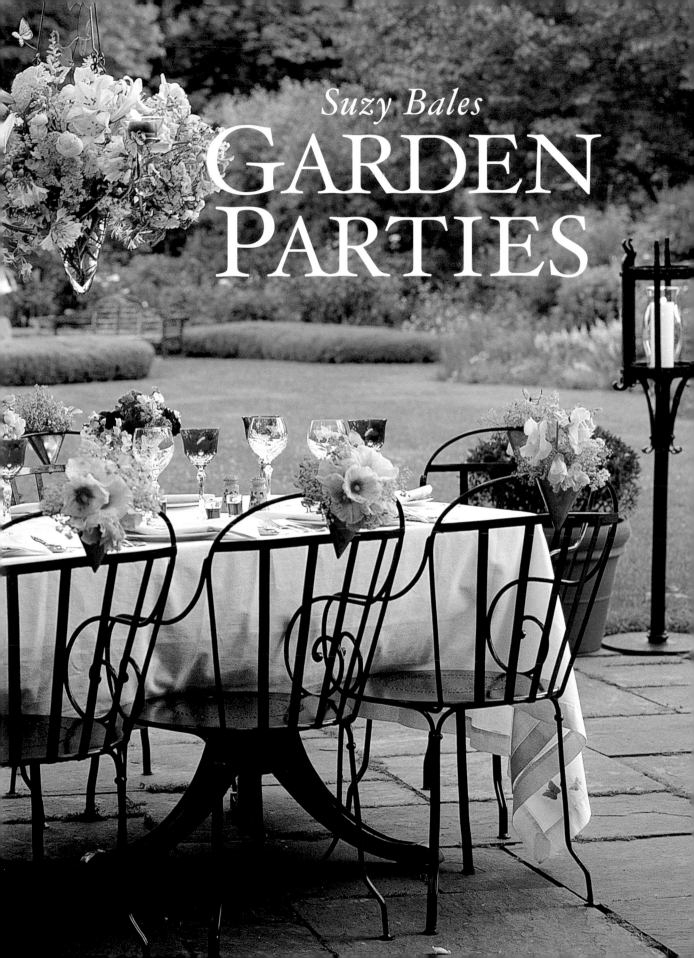

Suzy Bales

# GARDEN PARTIES

Also by Suzy Bales

*A Garden of Fragrance*

*Ready, Set, Grow!*

*Gifts from Your Garden*

*The Burpee American Gardening Series:*
*Vines, Roses, Container Gardening,*
*Bulbs, Vegetables, Perennials, Annuals*

Copyright © 2003 by Suzy Bales

Photographs copyright © 2003 by Michael Luppino, except on pages 16, 35, 37 bottom, 38, 43 bottom, 72 bottom left, 74 right, 94 bottom, and 143 right, which are copyright © 2003 by Suzy Bales

Published by Clarkson Potter/Publishers, New York, New York.
Member of the Crown Publishing Group, a division of Random House, Inc.
www.randomhouse.com

CLARKSON N. POTTER is a trademark and POTTER and colophon
are registered trademarks of Random House, Inc.

Printed in China

Design by Douglas Turshen

Library of Congress Cataloging-in-Publication Data
Bales, Suzanne Frutig.
    Garden parties / Suzy Bales; photographs by Michael Luppino. — 1st ed.
Includes bibliographical references and index.
1. Cookery.    2. Entertaining.    I. Title.
TX715.B213        2003
642'.4 — dc21        2002002943

ISBN 0-609-61024-4

10    9    8    7    6    5    4    3    2

to
Gina Norgard,
my right hand
and
often my left

contents

# introduction

ALMOST EVERYONE AGREES that everything tastes better outdoors. Flowers make people feel better; a garden soothes. Mother Nature's bounty, the freshest herbs, vegetables, and flowers, gives you a head start. Put it all together and you have a memorable garden party — a feast for all the senses.

Whether your style is laid-back or posh, a garden setting presents food at its best and entertaining at its most creative. Some gardens boldly invite you in, while others slowly reveal their charms. But each inspires its own style of creative entertaining, from formal flower gardens to such surprising places as a vegetable patch.

A garden party is an invitation to indulge fantasies and exercise creative opportunities. Trees hold their arms aloft to be draped with lights, hung with hanging baskets or candelabra. Flowers such as lilies, clematis, and rosebuds last for days out of water and can decorate a table, hang in nosegays on the backs of chairs, or be strung in garlands without wilting. Edible flowers are tasty treats and beautiful garnishes. Flower petals can be scattered on a table, strewn over a salad, or tossed on the ground to direct guests along a path. Garden furniture is easily rearranged — under the shade of a tree to avoid the afternoon sun, or in the open under the stars at night. Cooking on an open fire surrounded by guests is even cozier than entertaining in a country kitchen.

The unexpected takes people by surprise. Objects that traditionally serve one purpose will delight when used for another — a wheelbarrow as a buffet table, a birdbath to serve drinks, an urn as an ice bucket, flower wreaths on garden ornaments, and a plant stand filled with fruit. I have even served salads in flowerpots and dished them up with trowels.

Good, often simple food — food that requires little preparation while the guests are present — lets you enjoy your guests. Summer cooking takes advan-

LEFT: Varga crystal is etched with garden motifs, perfect for a garden party. OPPOSITE, CLOCKWISE FROM TOP: A basket of flowers with a sign directs guests to the party; a blooming salad; tricolor vegetable pâté.

tage of the fresh fruits, herbs, and vegetables of the season, making it easier to cook flavorful meals. On a hot night, food served chilled or at room temperature is a treat. And by preparing the meal well in advance, you can spend more time enjoying your party.

There are a few drawbacks to garden entertaining. But, on balance, the beauty of the garden, the fragrance of the flowers, the glow of the moon and the stars, especially after a day at the office, tip the scales. Remember, each potential problem has a solution. The most frequently expressed concern is bugs. Bug repellent is the common answer; citronella candles, another. I have also dragged out a portable fan to create a gentle breeze to discourage bugs from alighting on my guests. The distance from the kitchen to the outdoor table may also be a deterrent: A wagon, a wheelbarrow, a garden cart, even a picnic basket can solve the problem, allowing you to move more things at once. Any of them might double as a side table.

Recently, at a June dinner for ten, Mother Nature waved her magic wand and the stars lined up, the heavens were glorious, the temperature was in the mid-seventies, the bugs were banished by a gentle breeze, and the moon was perfect. Another June evening, the temperature took a plunge. So before the guests arrived I built a large campfire in a fire pot in the middle of the terrace and piled it high with logs. The five tables, each set for ten, were placed in a circle around the fire.

The bottom line is: Don't let anything stand in the way of your outdoor entertaining. There is nothing better. If it takes a little more effort than serving dinner in the dining room, it also gives a lot more pleasure to your family and friends. And, as in the old familiar saying, "We tire of the pleasures we take, but never of those we give."

In the spring, before the
trees leaf out, the woods
are as festive as young girls'
party dresses. Sunlight
streams down to awaken
an explosion of blooms.
The hills of this woodland
path are a panorama
of bright crayon colors, with
streamers of yellow
daffodils tying everything
together— their vibrancy
is uncompromisingly happy
after a long, dreary winter.

sunday luncheon in the garden

## the garden

THIS WINDING WOODLAND PATH peaks when the bulbs bloom. Spring is the easiest time to have a garden in full, all-out bloom. Bulbs are the most reasonable of creatures, obliging and easygoing. Planting bulbs is as close to a sure thing as a gardener ever gets. Each fall, plant daffodils, scilla, crocus, and other bulbs that naturalize into the ground, and they'll increase in number and beauty in subsequent years. To do spring its full justice, plant a symphony of different bulbs so blooms merrily come and go from the beginning of the season to the end. Plant them under the lawn, the ground-covers, the perennials, and deciduous trees and shrubs so they jump out all over the yard.

When the guests arrive at the garden gate, they are directed down the woodland path to the pond, met along the way with yellow daffs, primroses, forget-me-nots, pasque-flower, bleeding hearts, Virginia bluebells, and violets. A bird-bath beckons with a tray of drinks. Guests are encouraged to take a drink and pick flowers as they stroll to lunch.

The terrace is near a water-lily pond, adjacent to a stream, whose gurgle is background music to conversation, accompanied by the croaking of frogs. As the ripples smooth out, the water mirrors the trees and flowers, doubling the blooms on view. A small patch of watercress grows in the running water, producing plenty for spring soups, summer sandwiches, garnishes, and whatever else one might desire. In other parts of the yard, flowering trees are just beginning to bloom. So dessert is served on a bench that encircles a cherry tree awash in frothy pink petals.

A basket is filled to overflowing with the garden's blooms and set on a birdbath pedestal to direct guests to the luncheon. Daffodils bloom in the pachysandra, and a funnel filled with daffodils and kerria hangs on the garden gate.

WHO CAN RESIST the first flowers of the year? Spring arrangements of yellow, orange, and white daffodils pop next to the blues and purples of the tulips, pansies, lilacs, and hyacinths. Their scent, too, is intoxicating. Don't hesitate to pick huge bunches of flowers: It helps prune the shrubs and strengthen the bulbs for next year. For a party outdoors, use the spring garden's vivid, bold colors for flower arrangements. A punch of color that might clash or be overbearing indoors — deep purple lilacs and orange tulips, for example — is invigorating and lets the spirit soar outdoors.

Guests are welcomed at the garden gate, where an old wire funnel of yellow daffodils hangs and a large basket of flowering branches sits on a birdbath. A sign hanging from the basket directs them to walk the woodland path to where lunch will be served.

## BLOOMING BASKETS

Line a large rustic basket with a plastic bowl, and fill it with floral foam held in place by several pieces of florist's tape crossing the top and adhering to the sides of the bowl. As soon as the flowering cherry and almond are cut, smash the bottom few inches of their branches on a cutting board with a hammer. (Do this with all woody stems, because it allows the water to more easily flow up the stem to the blossom.) Plunge them into a bucket of warm water with floral preservatives, along with bunches of tulips, snowflakes, Virginia bluebells, hyacinths, and bleeding hearts. Leave them overnight in a cool place until ready to make the arrangement. You can pick the flowers two days before the party and arrange them the day before.

Daffodils ooze a sticky substance that could clog the stems of other flowers and prevent them from taking up water, thus shortening their vase life; so condition and set aside daffs in a separate bucket of water. If left alone overnight, they lose most of their milky sap and can then be added safely to a vase with other flowers.

ABOVE: A series of interlocking tubes softly curves down the center of the table, holding the day's garden picks—daffodils, lilacs, pansies, primroses, checkered lilies, and Virginia bluebells. A bird nest, nestled into a curve, holds chocolate eggs. OPPOSITE: A close-up of the blooming basket includes red and yellow tulips, pink and white bleeding hearts, white snowflakes, pink and purple hyacinths, and Virginia bluebells.

## HANGING BASKETS

*Hanging basket* is a loosely used term. Most store-bought baskets are made of white plastic, which you can forgo to create your own in a variety of planters including terra-cotta, ceramic, tin, copper, wire, and basketweave. They are most commonly bowl-shaped and hang freely in an open space, although some are available with flat backs and rounded fronts, or funnel shaped, to hang smack up against a wall.

There are so many different ways to hang flowers—on walls, gates, doors, or from trees—to add a festive atmosphere and to place their beauty, unexpectedly, at eye level. Hanging baskets can be planted to last a whole season or filled with bouquets of cut flowers for a special occasion.

The table repeats the floral display, with a handful of choice stems placed in a vase made of a series of interlocking tubes. They are deep and long, similar to chemists' test tubes, to hold water and to support the flowers' stems upright. Tubes can be added or subtracted to reach the proper length for each table. A similar effect can be achieved by scattering a series of small vases, bottles, or champagne flutes, each holding a few flowers.

The guests who are seated with their backs to the pond have a different focal point: a small copper funnel planted with clumps of Johnny-jump-ups on the trunk of a tree. The dessert table uses a darker color palette: Early lilacs, blue hyacinths, and dark red parrot tulips fill the air with their perfume and add a dramatic touch as they spill from a glass pitcher.

ABOVE: A wire funnel hanging on the gate holds a glass of water to support the large bouquet of late-blooming daffodils and kerria branches. OPPOSITE TOP RIGHT: Roger and Sharon Bales help their grandchildren pick daffodils and tulips. OPPOSITE TOP LEFT: A copper funnel planted with Johnny-jump-ups is hung at eye level behind the luncheon table to enliven the view; they will bloom for several months before they outgrow their pot. OPPOSITE BOTTOM: Flower-arranging staples.

## FLOWER-ARRANGING STAPLES

Flowers last longer if they're conditioned (see page 105) for six hours or overnight before they're arranged. Pick them two days before the party and arrange them the day before; it saves time on the day of the party. Be prepared with a cupboard of flower-arranging staples, so everything you need is at hand. Here are the most useful items:

- **ASSORTED** sizes of vases, bowls, and containers
- **BASKETS**
- **BUCKET:** nonmetal, for conditioning flowers
- **CHICKEN WIRE:** can be scrunched in the neck of a large vase and taped in place to hold flowers as they are arranged; also good for covering blocks of floral foam when making topiary forms
- **FLORAL CLAY:** a green sticky clay easily broken into small pieces to hold arrangements in place
- **FLORAL FOAM:** green foam in brick shapes that absorb water and hold flowers in place
- **FLORIST'S TAPE:** to hold floral foam in place
- **FLOWER-GATHERING BASKET** (also called a trug): low and long, to support long-stemmed flowers lying down
- **FLOWER PRESERVATIVES:** contain the nutrients for conditioning flowers
- **PLASTIC FLOWER TUBES** (water picks): to hold single flowers or several thin-stemmed ones for arranging
- **SCISSORS AND PRUNERS:** need to be kept very sharp for cutting flower stems and branches

*White Wine Spritzers*

*Creamy Watercress Soup*

*Mustard and Garlic Grilled Butterflied
Leg of Lamb with Fresh Mint Sauce*

*Asparagus Bundles with Chives
and Lemon Butter*

*Mashed Potatoes and Parsnips*

*Chocolate Indulgence with Candied Flowers
and Crème Anglaise*

MENU FOR 6

# sunday spring luncheon

NOTHING SAYS SPRING like lamb and asparagus, whether for Easter Sunday or simply a first outdoor garden lunch. The butterflied leg of lamb is served with a light mint sauce to bring out the best of its flavor. Parsnips add a bold bite to the mild mashed potatoes, a perfect pairing with the lamb. As a starter, watercress soup hits the spot, served either warm or cold, depending on the weather. The rich, sumptuous chocolate torte is a fine finish to any meal; chocolate desserts go with everything. The candied flowers are both decorative and delicious, and they can be made weeks ahead and kept for a year or more if protected from sunlight and moisture.

# white wine spritzers

*Spritzer* is the German word for a drink of Rhine wine and soda. Spritzers are light and festive, perfect for an afternoon or a warm summer night. Any dry white wine can be used, and rosé's cheery pink color and fruity flavor make it another good choice. It is better to refill each glass as needed rather than filling a pitcher, which might sit too long and become flat.

SERVES 6

- 3 lemons
- 1 bottle chilled white or rosé wine
- 2 bottles chilled sparkling water

Carefully peel the rinds from the lemons in unbroken spirals for garnishes, then halve each spiral. Fill each wineglass half full with ice. Pour the wine into each glass until it is one-third full, and top with sparkling water. Garnish each with a lemon twist.

# creamy watercress soup

Jane Greenleaf is known on the North Shore of Long Island for her delicious watercress soup, made with watercress picked fresh from her own pond. Watercress is a generous plant that needs to be regularly pulled up to keep it in check, and Jane welcomes friends and neighbors to pick it. Her wonderful watercress soup is equally good hot or cold, depending on the temperature of the day, and it can be made the day ahead and reheated.

SERVES 6 TO 8

- 3 large Idaho potatoes (about $2\frac{1}{2}$ pounds), peeled and quartered
- 6 scallions, white and green parts, coarsely chopped
- 9 cups chicken broth
- 6 cups firmly packed fresh watercress leaves
- 3 tablespoons unsalted butter
- 1 egg yolk
- $\frac{3}{4}$ cup heavy cream
- 1 tablespoon fresh lemon juice
  Salt and freshly ground black pepper to taste
- 6 pansies, for garnish (optional)

In a medium saucepan, bring the potatoes, scallions, and broth to a boil, reduce the heat to medium-low, and simmer until the potatoes are tender when pierced with a fork, about 20 minutes.

Wash the watercress thoroughly and remove the tough stems and roots. In a large saucepan, melt the butter. Add the watercress and cook over medium heat for 2 minutes, or until the leaves are wilted.

Allow the chicken broth, potatoes, and scallions to cool. In a blender, puree one third of this mixture with one third of the watercress. (Be careful: If the soup is too hot, it may splatter and burn you.) Return the puree to the saucepan and set aside. Repeat with two more batches.

In a small bowl, whisk together the egg yolk, cream, and lemon juice. Add to the soup and warm before serving. Or to serve cold, chill and add more cream if necessary to thin it. Season with the salt and pepper and garnish with the pansies, if using.

NOTE *Watercress* (Nasturtium officinale) *is a pungent herb rich in vitamins and minerals, including iron, iodine, and calcium.*

## FLOWERS FROZEN IN ICE CUBES

First wash the edible flowers with lukewarm water
and place each blossom in an individual ice cube compartment that is half full of water. Flowers float, so
if you fill the compartment to the top, that's where your
blossom will appear. To get it in the middle of the cube,
the flower has to be frozen first in the half-filled tray,
then, an hour or more later, add water to form the top
half of the cube. Use distilled water, which makes the
clearest cubes. If you use tap water, the cubes may be
cloudy when they're removed from the tray, but when
added to drinks they clear up nicely. Be aware that
pansies exude a blue dye when frozen that stains any
fabric it touches. Not so for the roses.

# mustard and garlic grilled butterflied leg of lamb with fresh mint sauce

A butterflied leg of lamb—with the bone removed and the meat opened up to one flat piece, about ¾ inch thick—cooks faster and is easier to grill, slice, and serve than a bone-in leg.

SERVES 6 TO 8

- ¼ cup extra-virgin olive oil
- 3 garlic cloves, minced
- 2 teaspoons chopped fresh rosemary or 1 teaspoon dried
- 2 rounded teaspoons Dijon mustard
- 1 4- to 5-pound boneless butterflied leg of lamb
- 1½ tablespoons salt
- ¾ tablespoon freshly ground black pepper
- 1 batch of Fresh Mint Sauce (recipe follows)

In a medium bowl, mix the olive oil, garlic, rosemary, and mustard to make a paste. Lay the lamb flat on a platter and season each side with the salt, pepper, and paste. Allow it to marinate for several hours, and up to overnight, covered in the refrigerator.

Prepare a grill to medium-high heat. Grill the lamb approximately 10 to 15 minutes on each side, until medium rare, with an internal temperature of 135°F. (The lamb can also be cooked under a broiler, 6 inches from the heating element, for about the same amount of time; check frequently to avoid overcooking.) Allow the cooked lamb to rest for 10 minutes before slicing and serving with the mint sauce.

## fresh mint sauce

This is a light and refreshing sauce that's very popular in England for serving with lamb. It isn't as heavy as mint jelly, and it adds a subtle mint flavor without overwhelming the lamb.

MAKES ½ CUP

- 1 tablespoon raw sugar (turbinado sugar)
- 2 tablespoons minced fresh mint
- 6 tablespoons white wine vinegar

In small heatproof bowl, mix the sugar, mint, and vinegar with 2 tablespoons boiling water. Let cool to room temperature before serving. The sauce can be stored covered in the refrigerator, but it should be brought back to room temperature before serving.

# asparagus bundles with chives and lemon butter

The young, thin shoots of asparagus that first poke through the ground in spring are the most tender and succulent. Asparagus is perishable and should be cooked the day it is picked, and cooked quickly; if it's overcooked it becomes an unattractive gray-green and loses flavor. When purchasing asparagus, be sure the stalks are crisp and the cut ends aren't dry. Refrigerate with its cut ends in water until time to cook.

SERVES 6

- 30 stalks (about 1½ pounds) thin asparagus, trimmed (see Note)
- 18 chives, braided for tying the bundles together (see Note)
- 3 tablespoons salted butter
- 1 tablespoon fresh lemon juice (from about ½ lemon)
  Salt and freshly ground black pepper to taste

Bring a large saucepan of salted water to a boil. Using tongs, lay the asparagus on the bottom and bring the water back to a boil for 3 to 5 minutes. Remove the stalks with the tongs when they are bright green and tender yet slightly crisp when poked with a fork. Thicker stalks might take a few minutes longer. Drain in a colander.

Place the asparagus on a serving platter and use the braided chives to tie bunches of 5 stalks together into individual servings.

In a small saucepan, melt the butter over medium-low heat. Stir in the lemon juice and mix thoroughly. Pour the hot mixture over the asparagus bundles and season with salt and pepper.

NOTE *To trim asparagus, hold a stalk with one hand lightly on its head and the other at its bottom; bend the stem and it will break apart where it begins to toughen. If the stalk is smaller than your baby finger, it doesn't need to be peeled. Otherwise, use a vegetable peeler to remove the outer layer of skin up to but not including the tip.*

*To braid the chives, cut eighteen 8-inch-long strands. Place three strand ends side by side, with ½ inch resting under a mug or another weight to hold them steady while the lengths are braided loosely together. First pass the right outside strand over the middle one. Then pass the left strand over the new middle, repeating until within ½ inch of the ends. Holding both ends of the chives, one in each hand, slide them under the middle of a bundle of 5 asparagus and tie the ends together in a knot.*

ABOVE: Pasqueflower, *Anemone pulsatille.*

## mashed potatoes and parsnips

This is a recipe that Tony Riolla, a friend and fellow ballet enthusiast, shared with me more than twenty years ago. The parsnips add a sharp flavor to the potatoes, and the combination is a perfect complement to the lamb.

SERVES 6

4 parsnips (about 1 pound), peeled and quartered
3 large Idaho potatoes (about 2½ pounds), peeled and quartered
Salt
¼ cup whole milk
4 tablespoons unsalted butter, melted
2 tablespoons sour cream

Put the parsnips and potatoes in a large pot with salted water to cover. Bring to a boil, then reduce the heat to medium and cook until tender when pierced with a fork, about 20 minutes. Drain in a colander. Puree the vegetables through a potato ricer into a large mixing bowl, or mash by hand until creamy-smooth.

Heat the milk in a small saucepan until tiny bubbles form around the outside of the pan. Mash the potatoes and parsnips with the melted butter and warm milk until they have a smooth consistency. Mix in the sour cream thoroughly and serve.

## chocolate indulgence with candied flowers and crème anglaise

Warm, gooey, rich, and luscious chocolate — the sweet sensation we can't get enough of. Jon Steves, a professional chef who catered many a party for the Joffrey Ballet, gave me this recipe. You may combine semisweet, bittersweet, and milk chocolates to suit your taste as long as the total amount stays at 12 ounces of high-quality chocolate. Whenever I make this recipe, I always make two — one to serve and another to freeze. Having a dessert or two waiting in the freezer spurs me to throw an impromptu party.

SERVES 10

- ½ pound (2 sticks) unsalted butter, cut into small pieces, plus extra for greasing the pan
  All-purpose flour, for coating the pan
- 1 cup plus ⅓ cup sugar
- 4 ounces semisweet chocolate, chopped into small pieces
- 8 ounces unsweetened chocolate, chopped into small pieces
- 5 extra-large eggs, at room temperature
  Confectioners' sugar, for sprinkling
- 1 cup whipped heavy cream or Chantilly Cream (optional, see page 138)
  Candied Flowers (recipe follows)
- 1 quart Crème Anglaise (recipe follows)

Preheat the oven to 350°F. Butter and flour a 12-inch springform pan, and wrap the bottom of the pan in heavy-duty aluminum foil to keep water from seeping in while the cake is baking.

In a heavy 1-quart saucepan, combine 1 cup of the sugar and ½ cup of water. Bring the mixture to a boil over high heat and cook for about 4 minutes, or until the sugar is completely dissolved and the mixture reaches 220°F. on a candy thermometer. Remove from the heat and stir in the chocolates until they are completely melted. Add the butter several pieces at a time and whisk until the mixture is smooth and shiny. Set aside to cool.

In the bowl of an electric mixer, beat the eggs and the remaining ⅓ cup of sugar on high speed for 10 to 15 minutes, until thick, pale yellow, and tripled in volume. Gently fold in the chocolate mixture. Pour into the prepared pan. Set the pan in a high-sided roasting dish and add water to the dish to a 1-inch level around the pan. Bake for 1 hour, or until a toothpick inserted into the torte comes out clean. Allow the torte to cool before removing the sides from the pan.

For decoration, place a round doily on top of the torte and sprinkle confectioners' sugar over it through a sieve. Remove the doily and, if desired, spoon on a mound of whipped heavy cream or Chantilly Cream and embellish with Candied Flowers. Serve with Crème Anglaise on the side.

## candied flowers

Many flowers can be candied and used as snacks or to decorate desserts, a practice that was popular in seventeenth- and eighteenth-century Europe. Violets, Johnny-jump-ups, scented geraniums, pansies, and rose petals are the most commonly used. The process is simple enough that children can do it: All you need is a gently beaten egg white, a small paintbrush, and superfine sugar. The color and shape will last for months or even a year if the flowers are stored properly.

MAKES 1 DOZEN

- 1 cup edible flowers (see box on page 30)
- 1 egg white
  Superfine sugar, for sprinkling

Rinse the flowers gently in cool running water and pat dry. In a small bowl, whisk the egg white. With a small clean paintbrush, paint each flower or petal with egg white on both sides; the flowers must be completely covered with egg white to prevent decay. Sprinkle both sides with superfine sugar.

Allow the flowers to dry and harden in a colander or on a clean screen where there is good circulation and low humidity. When dry, the blossoms will be hard and easy to move. Store in a sealed dark container, away from sunlight.

## crème anglaise

The most perfect vanilla custard sauce, Crème Anglaise goes with almost anything: over ice cream or berries, as one side of a hot fudge sundae, and especially as a topping for a chocolate soufflé or torte. It's easy to make and keeps well in the refrigerator in a closed container for several days. Make it the day before a party.

MAKES 1 QUART

- 3½ cups whole milk
- 8 egg yolks
- 1 cup sugar
- 1 teaspoon pure vanilla extract

Set ½ cup of the milk to chill in the refrigerator. In a heavy 2-quart saucepan, heat the remaining 3 cups of milk until small bubbles form around the edges. Remove from the heat.

Place the egg yolks, sugar, and vanilla in the bowl of an electric mixer and beat on high speed for 3 minutes, or until the mixture thickens. The mixture should be soft yellow, much lighter than the original egg-yolk color, and thick enough that when the beater is lifted the mixture ribbons back into the bowl.

Pour the egg mixture into the hot milk and return the pan to medium heat. Cook for 3 to 5 minutes, stirring constantly with a wooden spoon. (If you don't stir, it might overcook and the egg yolks could scramble.) When the sauce is slightly thickened and coats the spoon, test it by sliding your finger across the back of the spoon: If it leaves a mark in the coating for a few seconds, the sauce is done. Immediately add the ½ cup of cold milk to stop the cooking and start the cooling. Allow the custard to come to room temperature before placing it in an airtight container and refrigerating until ready to serve. Serve cold or at room temperature.

# EDIBLE FLOWERS

Edible flowers have been used for centuries in European and Asian cuisines: The Japanese cook daylilies, the Italians fry zucchini blossoms, and the French flavor food with rose water. Some flowers are similar to lettuce in not having much flavor, but many are very flavorful: The flowers of borage have a strong cucumber flavor, chive flowers add onion, honeysuckle is honey-sweet, and lavender is pungent. Violets, apple blossoms, lilacs, and some roses have a sweet floral taste. Nasturtiums have beautiful edible flowers with little flavor, but their leaves are very spicy and can be substituted for black pepper. Tulips have a crisp texture and taste similar to peas. (Make sure you remove the pollen and stigma from tulips before using; they don't taste good.) Consider rose petals or violets in salads, frozen in ice cubes, or floating in white wine or cold soup. Candied flowers decorate all kinds of desserts, especially wedding cakes.

| COMMON NAME | LATIN NAME | FLAVOR |
| --- | --- | --- |
| Anise Hyssop | *Agastache foeniculum* | anise with a hint of root beer |
| Apple Blossom | *Malus* species | sweet floral |
| Arugula | *Eruca vesicaria* | nutty with a hint of horseradish |
| Bee Balm | *Monarda didyma* | spicy and minty |
| Borage | *Borago officinalis* | light cucumber |
| Calendula | *Calendula officinalis* | tangy, slightly bitter |
| Chives | *Allium schoenoprasum* | onion |
| Chrysanthemum | *Chrysanthemum X morifolium* | bitter |
| Daylilies | *Hemerocallis* species | tasteless to sweet floral |
| Dill | *Anethum graveolens* | dill |
| Honeysuckle | *Lonicera japonica* | sweet |
| Johnny-jump-up | *Viola tricolor* | lettuce |
| Lavender | *Lavandula angustifolia* | pungent, lemon |
| Lilacs | *Syringa vulgaris* | range of sweet florals |
| Marigolds | *Tagetes* species | pungent to citrus |
| Nasturtium | *Tropaeolum majus* | pungent, peppery |
| Pansies | *Viola wittrockiana* | lettuce |
| Pinks | *Dianthus* species | spicy to floral and clovelike |
| Roses | *Rosa* species | fruity to spicy and floral |
| Runner Beans | *Phaseolus coccineus* | sweet, green bean |
| Scented Geraniums | *Pelargonium* species | sweet to floral/fruity to spicy |
| Society Garlic | *Tulbaghia violacea* | garlic |
| Squash Blossoms | *Cucurbita* species | slightly sweet |
| Tulips | *Tulipa* species | pea |
| Violet | *Viola odorata* | sweet floral |

In America, edible flowers are now available in many supermarkets. Yet the best way to obtain them is from your own garden, where the choices are many and they can go directly from the garden to the table. Not every flower is edible, however; many poisonous flowers are commonly grown, such as delphiniums, foxgloves, daffodils, and oleander.

Of course, not all edible flowers are tasty. Unless they have a fragrance, they won't have a flavor (but they can still make beautiful garnishes). Before cooking with a flower, taste it. Flowers with strong scents may be overpowering, so use them judiciously. Flowers with unpleasant scents are best not used at all.

Some flowers, nasturtiums for one, can be used whole; others, such as chrysanthemums and lavender, are better if only the petals are used. Roses have a hard core, so pull out the petals; the base of each has a bitter white spot and that, too, should be cut off with a paring knife.

Above is a list of edible flowers. For more information, check out *The Edible Flower Garden* by Rosalind Creasy, a leading expert, or contact your County Extension Office.

**A NOTE OF CAUTION** It is essential to use only pesticide-free blooms, preferably from a home garden or purchased at a grocery store, never from a florist. Florist-grown flowers usually have been sprayed with toxic chemicals.

If you need a reason to throw a party, look no farther than roses in bloom.

Luckily, we don't have to fall down a rabbit hole like Alice in Wonderland to enjoy a Mad Hatter tea party. The theme has been popping up everywhere from fancy New York hotels to children's parties, and since the Queen of Hearts ordered the roses painted

## mad hatter tea party

red, hosting one in a rose garden seems the only sensible thing to do.

MY LONGTIME FRIEND and neighbor Laurie Barry uses her garden as an outdoor room to host many events. As she says, "Every season has its own magical colors and light, but the moment the roses arrive, heralding the summer, their intoxicating perfumes fill our hearts and our home with love."

Laurie designed the garden to showcase her favorite flowers —roses and peonies. The peonies bloom first, and just as their numbers are waning, the roses begin. For a few all-too-short weeks, they bloom in synch, dazzling the eye with their full-blown beauty and tickling the nose with their sweet perfumes.

The rose garden is situated on the middle terrace of a three-tiered lawn, which slopes down from the house to the bay. The garden is laid out in six rectangular beds, three on each side of the terrace. The front two beds are devoted solely to rose bushes, totaling more than a hundred. The back beds, one on each side, are a mix of peonies and iris. A wide grass walkway with a central seating area runs down the middle. A hedge with a central arch encloses this terrace, offering a private seating area and framing the view of the passing boats on the water.

Through the arch and down the hillside, a mixed flower border surrounds a swimming pool and peeks out from behind a white picket fence. A gazebo draped in trumpet vine offers another view of the bay.

The bluestone terrace on the top level provides a 180-degree view of the harbor and the shore beyond—a spectacular sight, and the perfect place to welcome guests with drinks. A stone path leads to a small terrace off the kitchen, where a table piled high with food awaits; twining red roses and white blooming clematis flank the door and frame the table.

OPPOSITE: Champagne and Peach Sparklers and Pink Party Fruit Iced Tea await guests on the Barrys' terrace, with a spectacular view over the rose garden and down to the bay. An antique silver basket holds peonies and lilacs. ABOVE: Rosa 'Heritage' is one of the many fragrant roses Laurie grows.

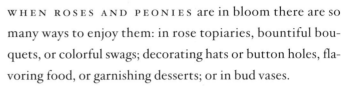

WHEN ROSES AND PEONIES are in bloom there are so many ways to enjoy them: in rose topiaries, bountiful bouquets, or colorful swags; decorating hats or button holes, flavoring food, or garnishing desserts; or in bud vases.

To decorate the seating area, we created a pair of mock topiaries embellished with pink, red, and apricot full-blown, old-fashioned roses accented with lime-green lady's mantle. The tall topiaries place the flowers at eye level and help them stand out.

Under an ivy-covered arch, we hung a basket of roses and peonies that added a welcoming spark of color to the dark green foliage. A flower garland by floral designer J. Barry Ferguson was hung behind the tea table. A bouquet of lilacs and peonies, both beautiful and highly fragrant, dressed up the drinks table. To continue the Mad Hatter theme, Laurie adorned her straw hat with flowers; guests were encouraged to do the same as they arrived.

OPPOSITE, CLOCKWISE FROM TOP RIGHT: A mock topiary of roses, alliums, and lady's-mantle; a basket of freshly picked roses and poppies; the ivy-covered arch is adorned with a hanging bouquet of roses and honeysuckle. ABOVE: Guests return from a walk to the beach.

## MOCK ROSE TOPIARIES

The topiaries are a play on "painting the roses red," a command of the Queen of Hearts in *Alice's Adventures in Wonderland*. Create them by inserting a 3-foot-long birch branch approximately 1 inch in diameter into a plastic pot (a deli container works) of wet plaster of Paris. The pot should fit snugly inside a decorative ceramic pot.

When the plaster hardens, place half of a brick of moistened floral foam, cut into a square, on the tip of the branch, then mold chicken wire around the foam to hold the flowers. Secure the chicken wire to the stem with green florist's tape.

Then insert pachysandra, an evergreen ground cover, into the floral foam to cover it before adding the flowers. Cut the stems short and poke them into the corners and edges, turning the square into a ball.

Remember to save the topiary forms once the flowers fade. Just remove the spent blooms and insert fresh greens and flowers for the next party.

## TO MAKE A SWAG

Floral designer J. Barry Ferguson shared his expertise and demonstrated how to make a swag or floral garland: First measure the length needed. (The main length of our swag was 9 feet long to drape across the windows of the pool-house doors; on each side was a 3-foot vertical fall.)

Twist together long lengths of bittersweet vine or heavy twine for the swag's frame. Lay the frame on the workroom table to the premeasured length. Barry clipped bunches of evergreens, Japanese holly, mountain laurel, and Korean boxwood on 8-inch stems from the nearby hedges and conditioned them overnight.

Starting in the center of the swag, tie the bunches of greens to the frame by winding a spool of lightweight (23-gauge) green wire around them and working out to each end of the swag. Cover the ends of each bunch with a new bunch and finish each end with a small loop of substantial wire for hanging.

Construct the pair of vertical falls in a similar way, leaving trailing greens at the bottom and a wire for hanging on the top. Keep the swag and falls on the cool concrete floor of the garage under multiple sheets of wet newspaper until a few hours before the party.

Water picks—green plastic tubes that are rubber-capped and pointed at one end—are the most important tools to make a swag. They are readily available from florists and craft stores. Fill them in a bucket of water, set the caps on, and poke them in a sheet of Styrofoam to stand them up. You can do this the day before.

Cut the flowers—we used roses and peonies in shades of white, cream, red, peach, magenta, and apricot—the day before and condition them (see page 105). The morning of the party recut them, leaving a 2- to 3-inch stem. Push each stem carefully into the hole in the rubber cap of a water pick. Replace the picks, standing upright, into the Styrofoam sheet and leave them in a cool place until the swag is hung.

The installation of this swag was easy because it was wired to the door hinges. In another place, a couple of cup hooks or strong nails might be needed to hang the swag and then the falls. A swag is also attractive gently curving down the center of a dining table with candles alternating alongside.

Once the swag is hung, add extra bits of green if needed to give it a full belly. The frame must be thick and firm to hold the flowers. Hold the greens with one hand and add the flowers with the other by carefully pushing a water pick into the foundation. (The pick points down so the water doesn't fall out.) Place the largest flowers in the center, creating a bull's-eye. Group the flowers as if you are painting with colors to create the overall look. Reinforce the shape by placing the flowers in clusters of color.

It's a good idea to hang the swag in a shady spot, out of the sun. The flowers last longer, usually into the following day.

You can create a simpler, thinner swag using a vine that easily lasts without water, such as bittersweet, ivy, or perennial sweet pea. Twisting together several lengths of the same vine is quick and easy for a more casual party. You can add flowers in water picks depending on the occasion. A lighter-weight swag could be draped along the side of a buffet table and pinned to the tablecloth at each end.

*Champagne and Peach Sparkler*

*Pink Party Fruit Iced Tea*

*Traditional Earl Grey Tea*

*Double-Decker Cucumber Sandwiches*

*Dill and Lobster Salad on Pumpernickel*

*Tarragon Chicken Salad in
Pâté à Choux Puffs*

*High-Hat Scones with
Devonshire Cream and Jam*

*Summer Berry Tartlets*

*The Queen of Hearts' Jam Layer Cookies*

*Painting-the-Roses-Red Miniature
Chocolate Cupcakes*

*Mushroom Meringues*

MENU FOR 16

# mad hatter tea party

TRADITIONALLY, a tea is served late in the afternoon at a time when nearly everyone craves a snack. Tiny sandwiches and mini desserts, like the Mushroom Meringues and rose cupcakes, are easy to make and fun to eat, and they shouldn't spoil the guests' appetite for dinner later.

It's best to offer an array of drinks, hot and cold. The Pink Party Fruit Iced Tea in a sugar-frosted glass is more festive than traditional iced tea. A Champagne and Peach Sparkler is perfect for toasting the hostess and signals that the event is pure fun and festive.

# champagne and peach sparkler

A Champagne and Peach Sparkler is a little different from a Bellini, which is made with white peach puree. The peach mixture can be made during the height of the fresh peach season and then frozen. The peach puree keeps in the refrigerator for a day or two.

SERVES 16

- 4 ripe peaches, peeled and sliced (reserve slices from 2 peaches for garnish)
- 2½ tablespoons sugar
- 4 teaspoons Grand Marnier
- 2 teaspoons crème de cassis
- 3 bottles moderate-priced champagne or other sparkling wine

In a small saucepan, cook the peach slices with the sugar over medium heat, stirring often, for 15 to 20 minutes or until soft. Puree in a blender or food processor. Set aside to cool before chilling in the refrigerator.

In a medium pitcher, stir the Grand Marnier and the crème de cassis into the cold peach puree. Spoon 1 tablespoon of this mixture into a fluted glass and top with champagne. Stir lightly and garnish with a peach slice.

# pink party fruit iced tea

Fruit-flavored herbal iced tea is refreshing on a hot day. It doesn't contain caffeine like most iced tea, so it's perfect for young children.

MAKES 2¾ QUARTS

- 8 wild-raspberry or strawberry-mango herbal tea bags
- 3 cups fresh orange juice (from about 8 oranges), plus orange slices for garnish
- ¼ cup sugar

Steep the tea bags in 2 quarts of boiling water for 10 minutes. Remove the bags and allow the tea to come to room temperature. Add the orange juice and sugar and refrigerate until cold. Serve over ice, each glass garnished with an orange slice.

# traditional earl grey tea

Earl Grey is the subject of legend: As the story goes, Earl Grey was the prime minister of England under William IV in 1830. One of his envoys in China saved the life of a mandarin, and to show his gratitude, the mandarin sent the earl a delicately scented tea made from a blend of large-leafed China tea; Darjeeling, an Indian tea; and oil of bergamot. This mixture has been known ever since as Earl Grey tea.

MAKES 1 POT OF TEA

- 3 to 5 teaspoons of Earl Grey tea
- Milk to taste
- Sugar to taste

There is an art to brewing tea. First, start with cold tap water that has been allowed to run freely for a minute or so to assure it is aerated. To bring out the best flavor, briskly boil the water. Pour a little into an earthenware or china teapot to warm the pot, then empty the water. Measure 3 to 5 teaspoons of tea according to taste into the warmed pot. Pour in the boiling water, cover the pot, and allow it to steep for 5 minutes; any shorter and the flavor will not develop, but too long and the tannin will start to emerge, making the tea bitter. Serve the tea alongside a teapot of hot water for guests who might like to dilute it.

## SUGAR-RIMMED GLASSES

Sugar-rimmed glasses can be used to serve almost any cold, sweet drink. They are simple to prepare and can be done several hours before the party. Colored sugar can be purchased at specialty food stores or can easily be made at home.

To make 16 sugar-coated glasses, you'll need 1½ cups sugar, food coloring, and 1 lemon, cut into wedges. Place ½ cup of the sugar in a clean glass jar. Add a single drop of food coloring, screw on the lid, and shake a few times to mix in the color. (A little food coloring goes a long way, so if the color is not as strong as you like, add another drop, no more, and shake it up.) Rub the rim of the glasses with a wedge of lemon, then dip the glass in the colored sugar. Allow it to dry for a few minutes before filling the glass. The lemon juice, when it dries, holds the sugar firmly in place.

LEFT: *Rosa mundi.*

# double-decker cucumber sandwiches

The traditional English cucumber sandwich has nearly transparent slices of cucumber served on lightly buttered bread as thin as a leaf. This double-decker version is from the Page Two Bakery in Oyster Bay, New York.

MAKES 20 TEA SANDWICHES

- 3   seedless cucumbers
- 3   tablespoons apple cider vinegar, for sprinkling
- 3   teaspoons salt
- 15  slices of seven-grain bread
- 8   tablespoons (1 stick) butter, softened
- 1   bunch of watercress; well cleaned, stemmed, and torn into sprigs

Peel off the skin of each cucumber if it is waxy. Thinly slice the cucumbers into a medium bowl. Sprinkle the cucumbers with the vinegar and salt. Set the cucumbers aside for 30 minutes, then dry them with a paper towel.

Slice off the bread's crust. Lightly butter one side of 10 slices, for the tops and bottoms of the sandwiches, and both sides of 5 slices, for the middle. To assemble the 5 large sandwiches, cover the buttered side of one slice with cucumbers and sprigs of watercress, top with a middle slice, cover with another layer of cucumbers and watercress, and finish with a third slice of bread, buttered side down. Cut each into 4 square tea sandwiches.

# dill and lobster salad on pumpernickel

Lobster salad is a summer extravaganza that most people can't get enough of. This simple salad can be served over lettuce for a light lunch, stuffed inside a ripe tomato for a first course, or stuffed in a grilled hot dog bun for a picnic at the beach.

MAKES 20 TEA SANDWICHES

- 1½  cups cooked lobster meat (from a 2-pound lobster)
- 2   teaspoons fresh lemon juice (from about ½ lemon)
- ¼   cup mayonnaise
- ¼   cup finely chopped celery (about 1 rib)
- 1   tablespoon chopped fresh dill
- ¼   teaspoon salt
     Freshly ground black pepper to taste
- 1   loaf of pumpernickel bread

Chop the lobster meat into small dice. In a medium bowl toss the lobster with the lemon juice. Mix in the mayonnaise, celery, dill, salt, and pepper.

Trim the crusts from 10 slices of bread. Spread the lobster mixture thickly on a slice of bread. Put a second piece on top and cut into 4 square tea sandwiches.

# tarragon chicken salad in pâté à choux puffs

This versatile chicken salad is equally at home served on lettuce slices, stuffed in a tomato, or between two slices of bread.

MAKES 24 PUFFS

- 4 boneless chicken breasts (about 1¾ pounds)
- ½ medium yellow onion
- 2 bay leaves
- ½ teaspoon salt
- ½ teaspoon freshly ground black pepper
- 2 tablespoons tarragon vinegar
- ½ cup mayonnaise
- 1 tablespoon chopped fresh tarragon or 1 teaspoon dried
- 1 tablespoon minced shallot
  Pâté à Choux Puffs (recipe follows)
- 2 heads Bibb lettuce, washed and separated

Place the chicken breasts, onion, bay leaves, salt, pepper, and 6 cups of water in a large pot. Bring to a boil, reduce the heat to low, and simmer for 20 to 25 minutes, or until the chicken is fully cooked and tender.

Remove the chicken from the water and while it is still warm chop it into bite-size pieces. Place it in a medium bowl and sprinkle it with the tarragon vinegar. Allow it to cool to room temperature, then dice it briefly in a food processor: Pulse 5 times, until the consistency is chunky yet easy to spread.

In a small bowl, mix together the mayonnaise, tarragon, and shallot. Pour over the chicken and mix well. Serve in Pâté à Choux Puffs sliced in half, with the lettuce.

# pâté à choux puffs

This is a basic recipe for choux pastry. It can be easily adapted into a cream-puff shell with the addition of 1 tablespoon of sugar sifted into the flour mixture. Cream puffs, filled with a scoop of ice cream and topped with hot fudge or another dessert sauce, are an all-time favorite summer treat.

MAKES TWENTY-FOUR 3-INCH SHELLS

- 1 cup sifted all-purpose flour
- ⅛ teaspoon salt
- ⅓ cup unsalted butter, plus 2 tablespoons for greasing the cookie sheet
- 1 cup whole milk
- 5 large eggs, at room temperature (see Note)

Preheat the oven to 400°F.

Sift together the flour and salt into a small bowl and set aside.

In a heavy medium pan over medium heat, melt the butter. Add the milk and bring the mixture to a boil over high heat. Add the flour-salt mixture all at once, and immediately stir it robustly with a wooden spoon until it becomes smooth and does not cling to the spoon or the sides of the pan. Do not overcook. Remove the pan from the heat and add the eggs one at a time, beating vigorously after each addition. The dough is ready to bake when it is stiff enough to stand up when pulled with a spoon.

Grease the cookie sheet with butter. Use a pastry bag or a tablespoon to drop the dough in rounds onto the sheet. Bake for 10 minutes, then reduce the temperature to 350°F. and bake for 20 minutes, or until the puffs are firm to the touch. Allow them to cool before slicing horizontally with a sharp knife and filling.

NOTE *If cold eggs are used, they may not cook properly because they are added when the mixture is off of the stove.*

# high-hat scones with devonshire cream and jam

Scones' taste and consistency fall somewhere
between the American biscuit and Irish soda bread.
They can be served warm or at room temperature.
For tea they are sliced open and spread with
Devonshire cream and jam. For breakfast I sometimes split and toast day-old scones before buttering
them. They are simple and quick to make, requiring
only gentle handling—quick mixing and gentle
turning, not kneading as with most breads. The
scones can also be cut in different shapes, as I did
for this party, using heart- and flower-shaped
cookie cutters. Scones are best baked the day they
are to be served, but they will be fine made a day
ahead and wrapped tightly in plastic.

MAKES TWENTY 2-INCH SCONES

- 1¼  cups all-purpose flour
- 1½  teaspoons sugar
- ½  teaspoon salt
- 4  tablespoons (½ stick) unsalted butter,
   cut into small pieces
- 3  tablespoons raisins
- ¾  cup buttermilk
   Jam
   Devonshire cream (see Note)

Preheat the oven to 400°F.

Sift together the flour, sugar, and salt into a
medium bowl. Mix in the butter with a pastry
blender or fork until the mixture resembles coarse
meal. Add the raisins and stir. Make a well in the
middle of the flour and pour in the buttermilk
all at once. With a spoon, quickly mix all the
ingredients until the dough forms. Turn out onto
a lightly floured surface, fold the dough in half,
and press down 4 or 5 times. Roll out the dough
evenly to a 1-inch thickness, about the width
of a finger. Cut into rounds with a 2-inch cookie
cutter, using a quick, sharp motion. Don't twist or
the scones will be distorted.

Place the scones 2 inches apart on an ungreased
baking sheet. Bake the scones in the middle of the
oven for 12 to 15 minutes, or until they have risen
and their tops are golden brown. Serve with jam and
Devonshire cream.

NOTE *If Devonshire cream—the English double, or
clotted, cream—is not available, try lemon curd, whipped
cream, or a mixture of equal amounts of each.*

# summer berry tartlets

The tartlet shells can be made several days ahead and quickly filled the afternoon of the party. They also freeze well and thaw quickly to be used on the spur of the moment.

MAKES 36 TART SHELLS

- ½ batch Jam Layer Cookie dough (recipe follows), refrigerated for 45 minutes
- 6 batches sabayon (see page 88)
- 12 ounces raspberries
- 8 ounces blueberries
- 1 pint strawberries, hulled and halved
  Confectioners' sugar, for sprinkling (optional)

Roll out the cookie dough evenly to ¼ inch thick. Line ungreased mini tart pans with the dough. (Use a 2½-inch round cookie cutter to cut dough for a 2½-inch fluted round tartlet pan.) Gently pat the dough into the pan. Trim any excess with a sharp knife. Chill in the refrigerator for 1 hour before baking.

Preheat the oven to 350°F.

Move the tart pans directly from the refrigerator into the oven. Bake for 5 to 7 minutes, or until lightly golden.

Cool and gently turn the shells over to remove the pastry from the molds. Fill each just below the rim with cold sabayon. Top a dozen with the raspberries, a dozen with the blueberries, and a dozen with the strawberries. Sprinkle with confectioners' sugar.

NOTE *The assembled tartlets are best eaten the same day. However, the sabayon can be made a day ahead and kept in a sealed container in the refrigerator. The pastry shells can be made several weeks ahead, baked, and frozen, wrapped airtight.*

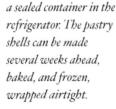

# the queen of hearts' jam layer cookies

This dough makes not only a delicious cookie, it also makes a sweet tart shell for summer berry tartlets. One recipe divided in half makes eighteen 2-inch jam layer cookies or twice as many 2½-inch tart shells. You can even make two different desserts at the same time.

MAKES 36 COOKIES

**Dough**
- 1 pound (4 sticks) unsalted butter, softened
- ¾ cup sugar
- 1 tablespoon pure vanilla extract
- ½ teaspoon salt
- 2 extra-large eggs
- 5½ cups sifted cake flour

**Topping**
- ¾ cup raspberry jam (1 teaspoon per cookie)
  Confectioners' sugar, for sprinkling

In the bowl of an electric mixer, cream the butter, sugar, vanilla, and salt until fluffy. Slowly mix in the eggs, one at a time, alternating with a third (about 1¾ cups) of the sifted flour. Divide the dough into 4 portions (for easier handling and rolling), wrap, and chill for at least 45 minutes.

Preheat the oven to 350°F.

On a lightly floured surface with a floured rolling pin, roll out half of the chilled dough evenly to ¼ inch thick (see Note). Use a 2-inch cookie cutter to cut the dough into circles. With a 1-inch cookie cutter, cut the center hole out of half of the cookies. (These centers can be baked and are delicious simply sprinkled with confectioners' sugar, or they can be rolled out together and cut into larger cookies.) Repeat with the other half of the dough.

Bake on an ungreased cookie sheet for 15 minutes, or until evenly light brown and firm. Cool.

Spread a teaspoon of jam on the round bottom cookies, then top with the cookies with the holes. Sprinkle with confectioners' sugar and serve.

NOTE *When pastry dough is made with butter, it softens quickly, making it difficult to work with; just pop it back into the refrigerator for a minimum of 20 minutes. A cold marble slab is the best surface for rolling out pastry.*

# painting-the-roses-red miniature chocolate cupcakes

Many cooks today have settled for cake mixes, and you can certainly substitute one here if time is short. However, chocolate cake made from scratch is ever so much better. Since the cupcakes freeze well, bake a large batch and save some for another special occasion.

The cupcakes are more memorable and festive when topped with a butter-cream rose, which can also be made ahead and frozen separately.

MAKES 5 DOZEN MINIATURE CUPCAKES
OR 24 REGULAR CUPCAKES

- 2 cups sifted all-purpose flour
- 1 teaspoon baking soda
- ¼ teaspoon salt
- ½ cup unsweetened cocoa (see Note)
- 10 tablespoons (1 stick plus 2 tablespoons) unsalted butter
- 1½ cups sugar
- 1 teaspoon pure vanilla extract
- 2 extra-large eggs
- 1 cup light buttermilk
- 1 batch of Chocolate Butter-Cream Icing (recipe follows)
- 60 Red Butter-Cream Roses (recipe follows)

Preheat the oven to 350°F.

In a medium bowl, sift together the flour, baking soda, salt, and cocoa.

In the large bowl of an electric mixer, cream the butter with the sugar. Beat in the vanilla. Use a rubber spatula to scrape the bowl as necessary to mix in all the ingredients. Beat in the eggs, one at a time.

On low speed, alternately add the sifted dry ingredients in three additions and the buttermilk in two. Continue to scrape the sides and mix only until the batter is smooth.

Line mini cupcake pans or mini muffin tins with 1½-inch cupcake liners (see Note). Spoon the batter (about 1 generous tablespoon) into the cupcake forms, filling them only two-thirds full. Bake for 20 to 25 minutes, or until the tops spring back when lightly touched. Allow the cupcakes to cool completely before frosting.

Frost with a thin layer of Chocolate Butter-Cream Icing and top with a Red Butter-Cream Rose.

NOTE *Use a high-quality Dutch cocoa such as Droste for the best flavor.*

*If you don't have cupcake liners, butter the forms and sprinkle with flour. The cupcake liners not only are a timesaver, they also give the cupcakes a dependable shape.*

## chocolate butter-cream icing and red butter-cream roses

Summer's heat and humidity make it difficult to keep butter-cream roses from melting. This icing is a variation on the traditional all butter recipe. The butter-flavored shortening gives the cream more stability so it holds its shape better, without sacrificing flavor.

MAKES FROSTING FOR 4 DOZEN MINIATURE CUPCAKES OR 24 REGULAR CUPCAKES, OR FILLING AND FROSTING FOR A 2-LAYER CAKE

- 1 pound confectioners' sugar
- 4 tablespoons (½ stick) unsalted butter, softened
- ¼ cup butter-flavored all-vegetable shortening
- 1 teaspoon pure vanilla extract
- 3 tablespoons whole milk, cold
- 1 ounce unsweetened chocolate
   Red food coloring

In the large bowl of an electric mixer, beat together the sugar, butter, shortening, vanilla, and milk until smooth. Begin by mixing slowly until the ingredients begin to blend, then increase the speed and continue beating at high speed until the mixture is creamy.

Divide the frosting evenly into two medium bowls.

Melt the chocolate slowly in a double boiler or over very low heat, stirring constantly until it is melted, smooth, and shiny. Stir it into one bowl of the frosting until blended, scraping the sides of the bowl if necessary.

Add a drop of red food coloring to the icing in the other bowl by dipping a toothpick into the coloring and then into the frosting; stir in with the toothpick. (It is easier to control the amount of color than if a dropper is used; a little color goes a long way.) Use a rubber spatula to finish blending in the color. Depending on how dark you want the color, continue to add color a little at a time, with a toothpick, blending completely after each addition. Keep in mind that the color darkens when the icing sits. Cover the red frosting with a damp paper towel and plastic wrap until ready to use.

To form the roses, fit a pastry bag with a number 12 tip and fill it half full of the icing. Twist the bag closed, forcing the icing down into the bag. A rose is easier to form on a cake decorator's rose nail. (A new, washed carpenter's nail works also, but don't tell anyone I said that.) Hold the nail in one hand and position the bag at a 45-degree angle with the wide end of the tip pointing down in the other. Squeeze the bag hard until the frosting starts to come out. Then keep the pressure steady and slow. First make a circle of icing around the nail, a half inch from its top. This will be the base of the rose. Now you must do three things at once: As you squeeze the bag slowly and consistently so a ribbon of frosting is flowing out, move the tip of the bag up from the bottom of the base to just above the nail, and then slowly back down again, releasing the pressure to the circle of frosting at the base, forming a petal. As you do this, slowly turn the nail, working your way around to form a layer of three petals. Repeat two more times, forming the second layer with five petals and the third with seven. (If you need to rest after forming a few petals, stop squeezing the bag and slowly lift it away.) Remove the rose from the nail by lifting it up from the bottom with a fork.

NOTE *For more detailed directions consult Wilton.com, the experts in cake decorating equipment and instructions.*

# mushroom meringues

Mushroom meringues are simple to make, although a little time-consuming. But they can be made ahead and kept without refrigeration for several weeks in an open container in a dry, dark place. An air-conditioned room is perfect in the humid summer. No need to worry if each mushroom is not flawlessly shaped—neither is the real thing.

MAKES 24 MERINGUES

- ½ cup egg whites (from about 4 large eggs), at room temperature (see Note)
- ¼ teaspoon cream of tartar
- 1¼ cups superfine sugar (see Note)
- 1 teaspoon pure vanilla extract
- ¼ cup milk chocolate chips
- 1 to 2 tablespoons cocoa, for dusting

Preheat the oven to 225°F.

Line two cookie sheets with aluminum foil, shiny side up. In the bowl of an electric mixer, beat the egg whites at medium speed until foamy, 1 to 2 minutes. Add the cream of tartar, increase the speed to high, and beat for another minute, or until the whites hold a soft shape. Add the sugar slowly, pouring ¼ cup at a time, as you continue beating on low. (If the sugar is added too fast, it will fly out.) Beat for 1 minute between additions. Add the vanilla, increase the speed to high, and beat for 7 to 8 minutes, until the meringue is very stiff and the sugar is dissolved. Don't let the meringue sit.

Choose a large pastry bag with a ½-inch opening and bend down the sides to form a large cuff. Fill the bag with meringue and then bend the cuff back up and twist the bag closed. To form the mushroom stems, hold the bag perpendicular to the cookie sheet. As you're applying pressure, draw the bag directly up 1½ inches. As you release the pressure, quickly pull the pastry bag away. To form the caps, hold the bag perpendicular ¼ inch away from the baking sheet, and squeeze so the meringue spreads out as it flows to form the round cap. When the cap is approximately 1½ inches wide, release the pressure and quickly pull the pastry bag away.

Bake the meringues for 50 minutes, then prop the door open and leave them to dry out further as the oven cools. (See Note.)

Once the mushrooms are cool, melt the chocolate chips in a double boiler to prevent them from burning. Stir until smooth (see Note).

If needed, use a paring knife to slice the narrow end of the stems flat for easy attachment to the cap. Spread the chocolate on the underside of the mushroom with a knife. Then immediately attach the stem's narrow top to the cap. The chocolate works like glue, holding the mushroom together as it cools and hardens. Place the completed mushrooms upside down on a paper towel to dry.

Place the cocoa in a strainer and gently shake over the caps and stems to give a "dirty" look. When the chocolate has hardened, the mushrooms are ready to be used. Store uncovered.

NOTE *Any time I make a recipe that calls for yolks and not the whites of an egg, I freeze the extra whites for use at another time. Separate egg whites when they are cold, but let them come to room temperature before beating them. A pinch or a scant ¼ teaspoon of salt is traditionally added to the egg whites, but I find it unnecessary and the recipe is just as good without it.*

*One cup of granulated sugar can be substituted for the 1¼ cups of superfine sugar. It does not give as smooth a texture to the mushrooms but is equally tasty.*

*Chocolate scorches easily, therefore it should never be melted over high heat. Melt it in a double boiler or over low heat, stirring constantly until melted, and remove from the heat and continue stirring until it is smooth and shiny.*

*Meringues should not stand any longer than necessary before baking. A sharp paring knife will gently shape or remove any points.*

## WEARING FRESH FLOWERS

Straw hats look wonderful with fresh flower accents. Cut flower stems short, about 2 to 3 inches, and insert them into plastic water picks filled with water. Tuck the picks into the hatband to hide them, or turn up the brim of the hat and secure it with a hatpin over the pick, allowing the flower to hang out. Or hide the pick with foliage; one large leaf might be enough.

To keep trumpet-shaped flowers (lilies, for example) fresh, moisten a tiny ball of cotton and tuck it into the center of the bloom. Another creative touch is to wrap the hat brim with trailing vines and let them hang down the back. You can also use a hat as a centerpiece or hang it on a wall to emphasize the Mad Hatter theme.

Flowers that last for a long time without water (passionflowers, lilies, flowering maple) and flowers that air-dry naturally (such as rose buds, hydrangea, and daffodils) need only be pinned in place. Experiment, be creative, and have fun.

ABOVE: Laurie Barry, in the white dress and wide-brimmed hat, chats with guests.

June, when days are long and nights are warm, is the perfect time to host a garden party. Imagine an enchanted evening, dining surrounded by flowers and friends enjoying the drama of the setting sun, then a garden awash in moonlight. I often entertain in my formal flower garden, although rarely are the parties themselves formal. However, I wanted this particular party to be

a midsummer night's dream

special, so I pulled out all the stops to bring together eight old and dear friends.

the garden

OUR HORSESHOE-SHAPED formal flower garden extends out from a large terrace on the side of the house. At the far end, the focal point is a rose garden and a reflecting pool with a fountain, backed by a holly hedge. The garden is enclosed on the two longer sides by five-foot-high stucco walls. In front of the walls, softly curved borders are filled to overflowing with annuals, perennials, and bulbs, backed by climbing roses and anchored by four vitex shrubs, one in each corner. It is a romantic and restful place with its pink, blue, and white color scheme.

Before the sun sets, the guests are seated at a table on the patio overlooking the garden. As dusk approaches, all along the borders the white flowers appear to move forward, glowing in the reflection of the moon—white roses, crinum and regal lilies, hollyhocks, flowering tobacco, and astilbe are all in the mix. The larger the flowers and the flatter their surface, the more light they catch and reflect. For example, the petals of hollyhocks are luminous, appearing to float in the air as all else recedes. Like candles in the dark, they flicker and twinkle in the reflected light. And many white flowers, lilies especially, spritz a floral perfume.

ABOVE: Willy and Ruta Jaget and Ray Knight arrive for the party. RIGHT: Hollyhocks.

THE ROSEBUDS, tucked into the invitation, are the guests' first indication that the evening will be special. Their second is the rose wreath that greets them on the garden gate, lush with assorted sizes and shapes of white, pink, and red roses on a background of deep green pachysandra. Through the gate, a small table holds an ice-bucket sculpture, ornate with flowers, chilling a bottle of champagne. An ornate three-foot-high birdbath masquerades as a fountain with hollyhock blooms floating in the water. In the center, a large four-tiered cake stand is piled high with hors d'oeuvres. Flowering sweet-pea vines twine up the pedestal, and the conversation flows as the guests gather around to sample the food.

The white color scheme, from the tablecloth to the flowers, reflects the moonlight. To add a sparkle, I set the table with crystal wineglasses, my best china, and polished silver that adds a luxurious touch to a garden party. The table sits under the welcoming arms of a century-old sycamore. From its branches a candlelit chandelier hangs suspended over the middle of the table. Its metal supports are wrapped with

## FLORAL FOAM RINGS

Floral foam rings (Oasis™ ring holders) are available in craft shops or from florists in a range of sizes. Hang one on a gate or a front door, or lay one on a table as a centerpiece. The centers of the largest rings could hold a single candlestick, a pillar candle in a glass chimney, or several votives. For a bit of whimsy, place them around the neck or on the head of a garden statue (see page 127).

Each ring is mounted on a sturdy but lightweight plastic tray, making it easy to handle. When using the ring on a table, set it on a plate to protect the table from moisture.

Saturate the ring by free-floating it, foam side down, in water mixed with a floral preservative. Cut the stems short on a sharp angle so they can be inserted easily into the foam without breaking. Poke the stems into the middle of the foam where they can take up water, not out the other side or touching the plastic. Cover the ring completely with foliage before adding the flowers to embellish it.

LEFT: A wreath of assorted roses and pachysandra hangs on the entrance gate.
ABOVE: Peeking out from a flower border, a hurricane candle sits atop a birdbath surrounded by floating hollyhock blossoms.

## COPPER FLOWER CONES

To make the copper cones, cut a sheet of thin copper into 9-inch circles. Cut the circles in half and gently bend each into a cone. Poke two small holes in the back of the cone, on each side where the copper overlaps. Insert a bit of wire through the holes to hold the cones together and allow them to be hung on the backs of the chairs. Cut triangles of moist floral foam and insert them into the cones. Poke the flower stems into the foam. If it is a hot day, keep the cones in a refrigerator until an hour or so before the party. Then hang one on the back of each chair as favors for the guests.

golden-heart ivy, and a trailing white blooming clematis dangles from its chain. In the center is a huge bouquet of white flowers — regal lilies, masterwort (*Astrantia major*), hydrangea 'Annabelle', 'Meiderland Alba' roses, Hall's honeysuckle, snapdragons, hosta flowers, and tall meadow rue (*Thalictrum polygamum*). Paper butterflies flit among the flowers. The chandelier hangs barely above the heads of the guests, so they can enjoy its fragrance.

At each end of the table is an antique celery glass filled with fragrant flowers, sweet peas and roses, to perfume the table. Tied to the back of each chair is a copper cone filled with a nosegay of hollyhocks and tall meadow rue.

Two birdbaths tucked among the flower borders hold pillar candles protected from the breeze by glass chimneys. The candles, surrounded by water and floating flowers, romantically illuminate the night.

TOP: A copper cone filled with hollyhocks and meadow rue hangs on the back of each guest's chair. OPPOSITE, CLOCKWISE FROM TOP RIGHT: A close-up of the candlelit chandelier with its bouquet of white lilies, masterwort, roses, hydrangea, hosta blooms, and variegated ivy; a swan planter holds double impatiens and petunias; flowering tobacco.

*Champagne Framboise*

*Seared Scallops on Rose Petals*

*Snow Crab in Pea Pods*

*Tricolor Vegetable Pâté*

*Persillade-Crusted Rack of Lamb*

*Potatoes Dauphinoise*

*Blooming Salad
with Saint-André Cheese*

*Apricot and Vanilla Baked Alaska*

MENU FOR 8

# midsummer's eve party

FOR SPECIAL OCCASIONS, an elegant three-course dinner is a must. Enticing hors d'oeuvres start things off deliciously. An easy vegetable pâté makes a great first impression and tastes as good as it looks. Everyone loves potatoes paired with succulent lamb chops, and a salad sprinkled with edible flowers pleases even the fussiest guests. For dessert, go all out: A baked Alaska finishes a memorable evening.

# champagne framboise

Whenever we serve Champagne Framboise we are reminded of good times on the terrace of the Hôtel Belles Rives in Juan-les-Pins, France. This summer drink is prettier and tastier than pink champagne or a kir royale, although I'd never turn either one away.

SERVES 8 (2 GLASSES PER PERSON)

- **2 pints raspberries**
- **2 bottles chilled champagne**

Rinse the raspberries and allow them to dry on a paper towel for a few minutes. Set aside 16 raspberries for garnishing the drinks. Puree the rest in a blender and strain them through a sieve to remove the seeds. Place 1 teaspoon of raspberry puree in the bottom of each champagne flute, then fill with champagne. Garnish each glass with a whole raspberry, either dropped directly into the glass or suspended across the top with a toothpick.

## BIRDBATH HORS D'OEUVRE STAND

This ornate cement birdbath is pressed into service to present the hors d'oeuvres, as if they are floating in a fountain surrounded by flowers. A tiered cake stand is set in the middle of the water, with plate-size blooms of hollyhocks floating around its base. The middle levels are filled with food just before the guests arrive. The bowl on the top tier holds a cluster of starry blue flowers, *Brodiaea coronaria,* cut from the garden.

The birdbath's base is dressed to look as if a garden is growing up from its feet. A floral foam ring (see page 57) is sliced open on one side and slipped over the base of the pedestal. Sprigs of myrtle on short stems are poked in to completely hide the foam. Perennial sweet peas on long limbs, conditioned and refrigerated overnight, are poked into the ring. To hold the sweet peas up as if they are climbing, the tops of the stems, flowers, or leaves are tucked underneath a thin, nearly invisible wire twisted loosely around the top of the column. The birdbath garden was assembled the day before the party and placed in a shady spot to allow us to concentrate on the food the day of the event.

# seared scallops on rose petals

Some guests will only use the rose petals to keep their fingers clean as they eat the scallops, and that's okay. More adventurous souls will discover that fragrant rose petals are tasty as well as beautiful. Depending on the rose, they may have a fruit flavor ('New Dawn' is apple) and a spicy taste ('Hansa' is anise and cloves), or they may be simply sweet, as in 'Seagull'.

SERVES 8 (2 PER PERSON)

- 8 medium sea scallops, halved crosswise
- 16 3-inch-long sprigs of dill
- 16 fragrant red or pink rose petals
- 3 tablespoons extra-virgin olive oil

Rinse the sea scallops, dill, and rose petals in cool water and pat dry on a paper towel. Snip out the white spot at the base of each petal (it is bitter).

Heat the oil in a large, heavy skillet over medium-high flame. Add the scallops to the hot pan and sear until golden brown, 1 to 2 minutes per side. Blot each cooked scallop on a paper towel and wrap a sprig of dill over the top and down each side. Place each scallop on a rose petal. They can be served immediately or allowed to cool to room temperature.

# snow crab in pea pods

In summer, this crabmeat spread is refreshing served chilled or at room temperature, atop Bibb lettuce as a luncheon salad or as an open-faced sandwich. It can be served in tartlets, in mini fillo shells, on crackers, in sandwiches, or stuffed in snow peas. The bright green of the snow pea is a perfect color complement to the white crab, and the stuffed pod can be picked up and eaten without making a mess.

Snow crab shreds easily and mixes well with the other ingredients in this recipe, but another crabmeat may be substituted.

SERVES 8 (3 PER PERSON)

- 2 dozen snow pea pods
- 1 pound snow crabmeat
- 4 tablespoons minced yellow onion (from 1 small onion)
- 5 tablespoons mayonnaise

Rinse the pea pods and remove the string from each. Bring a medium pot of water to a boil, add the pods, and blanch for 1 minute; remove the moment they turn a bright green, place in a colander, and rinse under cold water to stop the cooking. Pat dry with paper towels.

In a small bowl, mix the crabmeat, onion, and mayonnaise. Split each pod along its inside seam and stuff with the crabmeat mixture. Cover and refrigerate until ready to serve.

# tricolor vegetable pâté

This pâté is as beautiful as it is tasty. A serving, the size of a slice of bread, has alternating white and green layers topped with a decorative stripe of tomato cream sauce. It's an elegant first course for a dinner or a main course for a luncheon, served alone or with cold shrimp on the side. It can be made the day before and reheated for 20 minutes in a water bath before serving, or it can be assembled the day before, refrigerated, and then baked an hour before the guests arrive. Serve it warm or at room temperature.

SERVES 8 TO 10

- 4 tablespoons (½ stick) butter, plus additional for buttering the pan
- 4 leeks
- 3 tablespoons salt
- ½ small head of cabbage, cored and quartered
- 3 10-ounce bags of triple-washed fresh spinach or 3 10-ounce packages of frozen chopped spinach, defrosted, stemmed, and rinsed
- 2 cups chopped yellow onion (about 2 medium onions)
- 4 large eggs
- 1 cup heavy cream
- ⅓ cup grated Swiss cheese, plus 3 tablespoons for sprinkling
  Freshly ground black pepper to taste
- 2 pinches of cayenne pepper
- 1½ cups Creamy Tomato Sauce (recipe follows)
- 10 nasturtium flowers and 30 small leaves, for garnish (optional)

Preheat the oven to 375°F.

Lightly butter a 9 × 5 × 2¾-inch loaf pan. Line it with aluminum foil, the shiny side out, and thoroughly butter it again. (This will assure that the pâté is easily removed from the pan and holds its shape.)

Coarsely chop the bottom of the leeks, including the first 2 inches of green. Separate the rings and soak them in a water bath for a few minutes to remove all the soil hiding between the rings. Rinse again.

Bring a large pot of water and 2 tablespoons of the salt to a boil over high heat. Add the cabbage and cook for 20 minutes, until tender when poked with a fork. Drain and rinse under cold water. When cool, squeeze out the water with your hands. Coarsely chop the cabbage and leeks together by hand or in a food processor. Wrap them in a clean kitchen towel and squeeze out any excess water. Set aside in a medium bowl. You should have approximately 4 cups.

If using fresh spinach, bring another pot of water with the remaining tablespoon salt to a boil over high heat. Add the spinach and cook for 2 to 3 minutes, until the leaves are a bright green. Drain and rinse under cold water. Dry in a clean towel, and coarsely chop by hand or in a food processor.

In a medium pan over low heat, sauté the onions in the 4 tablespoons of butter until wilted and translucent, 3 to 5 minutes. Remove half the onions and add them to the cabbage-leek mixture. Add the spinach to the other half in the pan, increase the heat to medium, and sauté for 3 minutes, or until most of the moisture is removed. Set aside to cool.

In a small bowl, whisk together the eggs and cream until smooth. Divide it evenly between the spinach and the cabbage-leek mixtures. Add the ⅓ cup of grated cheese to the cabbage-leek mixture. Season both mixtures to taste with salt, pepper, and a pinch of cayenne.

The pâté has four layers. First evenly spread half of the cabbage-leek mixture, then add a layer of half of the spinach mixture. The third layer is the remaining cabbage-leek mixture, and the fourth is the rest of the spinach.

Place the loaf pan in a roasting pan filled with water to two thirds the depth of the loaf pan. Bake for 1 hour, or until firm and lightly brown.

Allow the pâté to cool for 30 minutes before unmolding. Turn the pan upside down on an ovenproof platter. If some liquid runs out on the platter, wipe it up with a paper towel. Pour half of the Creamy Tomato Sauce over the top of the loaf and sprinkle with the remaining 3 tablespoons of grated cheese. Place under the broiler for a few minutes, until the cheese bubbles and turns golden.

Slice the loaf like bread into ½-inch-thick pieces. Ladle a swath of Creamy Tomato Sauce across the middle of each slice and garnish with a nasturtium.

## tomato sauce

This all-purpose sauce is a basic for pasta, lasagne, veal Parmesan, you name it. It seems a waste of time to make any less than 2 cups, even though only 1 cup is needed for the Creamy Tomato Sauce topping for the pâté. I usually make three times as much, since the extra is easily frozen for another day.

MAKES 2 CUPS

- 1 large yellow onion, thinly sliced
- 4 tablespoons extra-virgin olive oil
- 1 28-ounce can whole Italian plum tomatoes, quartered
- 1 tablespoon minced garlic (about 3 garlic cloves)
- 1/3 cup minced fresh basil
- 1 teaspoon minced fresh parsley
- 1 teaspoon salt
- 1/8 teaspoon freshly ground black pepper

In a large saucepan over low heat, sauté the onion in the oil until soft and translucent, not brown or crisp, about 5 minutes. Add the tomatoes, garlic, basil, parsley, salt, and pepper and continue to cook over low heat until thick, about 30 minutes. Cool for 30 minutes to prevent spattering, then puree in a blender or food processor.

## creamy tomato sauce

MAKES 1 1/2 CUPS

- 1 cup Tomato Sauce (at left)
- 1 cup heavy cream

In a small saucepan over high heat, boil the heavy cream to reduce it by half. Strain the tomato sauce and add it to the reduced cream.

# persillade-crusted rack of lamb

A persillade, a simple mixture of finely chopped garlic and parsley, adds such a great flavor to the lamb that any additional sauce is unnecessary. This recipe is simple to prepare, allowing you to spend more time making dessert or an elaborate first course.

SERVES 8 (2 RIBS PER PERSON)

- 2 racks of lamb, each with 8 ribs
- 1 teaspoon salt
- ½ teaspoon freshly ground black pepper
- 4 large garlic cloves, minced
- 3 tablespoons olive oil
- 1 cup chopped fresh curly parsley
- 1 cup plain bread crumbs

Preheat the oven to 350°F.

Pat the lamb dry and season with the salt and pepper. Place the lamb in a roasting pan.

In a medium skillet, sauté the garlic for 3 minutes in 2 tablespoons of the olive oil, until soft and translucent but not brown. Remove from the heat and mix in the parsley and bread crumbs. It should have the consistency of a paste; if it is too thick to spread, add a little more olive oil. Set aside.

Roast the lamb for 15 minutes. Remove from the oven and pat the paste on all sides. Return to the oven and roast until a meat thermometer reads 150°F. for medium-rare, or 160°F. for medium; lamb has the most flavor at medium-rare. Let it rest for 10 minutes before carving it into separate chops, serving two per person.

NOTE *Cold rack of lamb, French-trimmed so it cuts easily into cutlets that can be eaten with your fingers, is a great treat on a picnic.*

# potatoes dauphinoise

Too rich to serve too often, Potatoes Dauphinoise are a special treat for a dinner party. The cheese and cream bake into a rich custard around the potatoes. Guests always request seconds. My sister, Jayne Mengel, perfected this recipe.

SERVES 8 TO 10

- 1 garlic clove, peeled
- 6 tablespoons unsalted butter, softened
- 6 large Idaho potatoes
  Salt and freshly ground black pepper to taste
- ¼ teaspoon nutmeg (preferably freshly ground)
- 2 cups (approximately ½ pound) grated Gruyère or Jarlsberg cheese
- 2¼ cups heavy cream

Preheat the oven to 350°F.

Rub an 11 × 16 × 1-inch jelly-roll pan with the garlic clove, then with 2 tablespoons of the soft butter. Peel and thinly slice the potatoes into a bowl of cold water. Drain and pat dry with paper towels. Spread over the bottom of the pan, generously overlapping the potatoes. Season to taste with salt, pepper, and nutmeg. Dot the remaining 4 tablespoons of butter evenly over the top, and sprinkle the grated Gruyère evenly, making sure to get it in the corners. Drizzle the heavy cream over the top.

Bake for 45 minutes, or until the cheese is golden brown and the potatoes are crispy. The potatoes can be cut into square portions and are easily lifted out with a spatula. Serve hot, straight from the oven.

## SCULPTURED ICE BUCKET

For special occasions, freeze flowers in a bucket of ice to chill white wine or champagne (see photo on page 60). You'll need two plastic buckets, one 6 inches larger in diameter. The smaller bucket must be large enough to hold a bottle of champagne or several wine bottles, as you prefer.

Fill the small bucket with rocks so it stays put and place it in the larger bucket. The water and flowers are added in three stages. First place a handful of flowers between the two buckets circling the bottom. I used roses, sweet peas, and pansies; ferns and other foliage can be added as background. To keep the flowers from floating to the top, cover them with crushed ice. Fill the space between the buckets a quarter full of water and allow it to freeze for a few hours or overnight. Repeat twice more, each time adding more flowers, foliage, and water; allow each layer to freeze before adding the next. Remember, water expands as its freezes. If the outer bucket is more than three quarters full, it might overflow into the inside bucket and freeze, making it difficult to remove the center without damaging your sculpture.

To unmold, remove the rocks from the smaller bucket, pour in a little hot water, let it stand for a minute, and turn it upside down in the sink. The small bucket should slide out easily. Next run warm water over the upside-down larger bucket for a few seconds, and the ice sculpture will slide out of the bucket. Once free, it can be used immediately or placed on a tray and returned to the freezer until needed. Always place a tray under the ice to catch water as it melts over the course of the evening.

LEFT: Catie Bales sips champagne with Katie Hirschfield and Ruta Jaget.

# blooming salad
## with saint-andré cheese

The ingredients in my blooming salads change
weekly, depending on what's in bloom in my
garden. In general, the smaller the flower, the more
of it can be used. Also, with the more pungent flowers such as lavender, a little goes a long way. A salad
can be wonderful with only one kind of flower, such
as violets. Even three flowers per salad enliven its
taste and appearance. See page 30 for more
information on edible flowers.

SERVES 8

- 3 heads Bibb lettuce
- 3 heads endive
- 24 small nasturtium leaves (see Note)
- 8 nasturtium flowers, one for each salad plate
- 32 Johnny-jump-ups or violets
- 24 fragrant rose petals
- 3 tablespoons chopped chives
- 1 batch Vinaigrette (recipe follows)
- 1 small wheel (about 1¼ pounds)
  Saint-André cheese

Rinse the lettuces and flowers in several changes of
cool water. Spin them dry in a salad spinner. With a
sharp knife cut the white tip (the place where the
petal was attached to the stem) off the bottom of
each rose petal; it can be tough and bitter. For the
most attractive presentation, arrange the salad on
individual plates with the Bibb and endive lettuce
on the bottom and the nasturtium leaves, chives,
and flowers on top. Dress the salad with the
vinaigrette immediately before it is served, and add
a sliver of cheese on the side.

NOTE *Caution: Always check whether a flower is indeed
edible before tasting it. Some flowers are poisonous—
foxglove, daffodils, and sweet peas, to name a few. Never
eat flowers that have been sprayed with chemicals such as
pesticides or fungicides. Flowers from a florist fall into this
category. Many gourmet food markets and some supermarkets now sell packages of edible flowers.*

## vinaigrette

MAKES ¾ CUP

- ¼ cup fresh lemon juice (from about
  ½ lemon)
- ½ cup extra-virgin olive oil
- 1 teaspoon Dijon mustard
- 1 large garlic clove, minced
  Salt and freshly ground black pepper to
  taste

Place the lemon juice, olive oil, mustard, and garlic
together in a screw-top jar and shake vigorously
until it is blended thoroughly. Season with salt and
pepper and shake again. This dressing will keep in
the refrigerator for several days.

# apricot and vanilla baked alaska

Much simpler than it sounds; even a beginner can make it. Baked Alaska is the most elegant American dessert. Although baking ice cream in the oven sounds implausible, the meringue insulates the ice cream, protecting it from the heat. Any leftovers, a rare possibility, can be covered and kept in the freezer. I guarantee they won't last past the next morning's breakfast.

SERVES 8 TO 10

- 2 tablespoons unsalted butter, softened, for greasing the pans
- ½ cup all-purpose flour, plus more for dusting the pans
- 4 eggs, separated
  Pinch of salt
- 1 cup granulated sugar
- ½ teaspoon pure vanilla extract
- ⅓ cup apricot or raspberry preserves
- 3 pints vanilla ice cream, slightly softened
- 1 cup (about 8 large) egg whites
- ¼ cup superfine sugar

Preheat the oven to 400°F.

Line the bottom of two 10-inch springform cake pans with aluminum foil. This helps to remove the slim layers without damage. Grease the bottom and sides of the pans with the butter, sprinkle with flour, and tip the pans from side to side to spread the flour evenly. Turn each pan upside down and tap it to dislodge the excess flour.

In a mixing bowl, beat the egg whites and salt until they form soft peaks (see Note). Add ¼ cup of the granulated sugar, 2 tablespoons at a time, and continue beating until the whites form solid peaks when the beaters are lifted out of the bowl. In a small bowl, beat the 4 egg yolks with a whisk until they are smooth. Stir in the vanilla. Fold a large spatula full of whites into the yolks, then fold the yolks back into the bowl of whites. Add the ½ cup of flour, 2 tablespoons at a time.

Divide the cake batter into the two pans, spreading evenly with a spatula. Bake in the preheated oven for 8 to 10 minutes, until the cake lightly browns and draws slightly away from the sides of

the pan. Let cool. Remove the cakes from their pans. Spread a thin glaze of apricot preserves on one cake and place the other cake on top. Wrap the cakes in foil to prevent drying until ready to serve.

To shape the ice cream, it needs to be slightly softened, approximately 10 minutes out of the freezer. Line one 10-inch round pan with 2 strips of aluminum foil criss-crossed and extended well over each side of the pan, leaving enough room to wrap up the molded ice cream. Press the softened ice cream into the pan with a spatula, shaping it into a slightly mounded center. Wrap it tightly in the foil, and place it in the freezer until needed.

Ten minutes before serving, preheat the broiler to its highest temperature. Beat the cup of egg whites until they form soft peaks. Slowly add the remaining ¾ cup sugar while continuing to beat the whites until they are shiny and stiff. (Too much beating causes them to become dull and grainy.)

Spread a 20-inch length of aluminum foil on a cookie sheet; the extra foil on the sides serves as handles to help move the cake onto its serving platter. Place the cake in the center. Remove the ice cream from the freezer and place it on top of the two layers of sponge cake. Frost the cake with the meringue, mounting it higher on top than on the sides, and use your finger to swirl and form peaks on the top. Sprinkle the ¼ cup superfine sugar evenly over the top and sides. Slide the cake under the broiler for 2 to 3 minutes and don't take your eyes off of it. Once the meringue turns a pale golden brown, remove it and serve it at once.

NOTE *Successful beating of the egg whites depends on several things. The bowl and beater must be squeaky clean, with no trace of grease, egg yolks, or oil. The egg whites must be at room temperature; if they are chilled they don't stand up properly. And lastly, don't overbeat: The best meringues stand tall, smooth, and shiny, but overbeaten egg whites are dull and grainy. If this happens, add another egg white and it will restore them to their former glory without hurting the taste.*

Some gardens are created for entertaining, such as Dennis Schrader and Bill Smith's tropical paradise. Paths beckon visitors from the house, and everyone immediately races off in all directions to explore. The paths start out straight, then meander, concealing one part of the garden from another, affording an element of surprise. At this party for twenty, it makes perfect sense to place food

strolling cocktail party

in different areas so guests, as they wander, are always close to a nibble.

the garden

THE GARDEN HAS EVOLVED from open farmland to a trendsetting study of flowers and foliage. Tropical plants in hot colors of orange, red, and yellow fire up the borders; plants with huge leaves, boldly colored foliage, and ferny textures dominate, their architectural beauty striking from a distance. This is no English country garden, but instead looks more like a rain forest in the Northeast. (The garden's style was popularized in *Hot Plants for Cool Climates,* written by Dennis Schrader and Susan A. Roth and published in 2000.)

The entry is a knot garden made up of boxwood, germander, and two contrasting colors of barberry, burgundy and green. A deck covered with pots of tender and tropical plants offers an expansive view of the grasslands beyond, or down the steps to a wide-open lawn that leads to the many garden rooms. A terrace next to the deck is often called into service as a dance floor.

As guests move from the terrace through the gardens, they encounter many surprises. The hot tropical colors of the far border give way to subtle and soft colors around the pond. The flower borders softly curve to lead past one of the many water gardens replete with hardy water lilies in a mass of blooms. Around one bend, a tiki hut is discreetly hidden by a grove of bamboo, trees, and shrubbery, reinforcing the illusion of being in a tropical garden. Throughout the garden banana trees, elephant ears, giant ferns, palms, and Amazon lilies are combined in bold and daring color combinations. Ornamental grasses, lush vines, perennials, and hardy water lilies add to the mix. While wandering, visitors might see lizards (rescued from a vacant New York City lot) sunbathing lazily on rocks, or the world's happiest rabbits nibbling on the plants.

ABOVE: The grasslands beyond the garden. OPPOSITE TOP: The urns in the knot garden entrance are filled with ice to cool the drinks. OPPOSITE BOTTOM LEFT AND RIGHT: The water lily pond; pots of succulents, pineapple lilies, and tropical plants are clumped together on the deck.

Bill and Dennis specialize in tropicals, and most gardeners grow them in some form, many without knowing it. Impatiens, begonias, coleus, and geraniums are just a few of the common ones. But Bill and Dennis have expanded the list with quick and inexpensive growers such as datura, amaranth, cannas, and caster bean that go from seed to over five feet tall in one season. They have opened the eyes of many visitors to the unlimited possibilities of designing with tropicals and playing with energizing colors.

ABOVE LEFT: Bill Smith takes guests for a stroll through his gardens. ABOVE RIGHT: Green bananas ripen in the tiki hut. OPPOSITE: The hot, fiery colors of the tropical border include orange canna lilies, the burgundy foliage of amaranth, yellow sunflowers, orange marigolds, and speckled coleus.

THE GARDEN ITSELF is the main attraction, so no elaborate flower arrangements are necessary. (But one of the guests, floral designer José Zavala, showed up with a bouquet of lady's-slipper orchids, which are the perfect touch for the elephant saddle table in the tiki hut, where dessert is served.) The garden lends its charm to the food as banana leaves, fern fronds, and ornamental grape leaves are placed as doilies under the food. At the same time, they line the baskets and platters for easier cleanup.

Bill keeps a vase of freshly picked basil handy on the kitchen table for cooking and salads, which makes a fragrant arrangement for the table overflowing with colorful vegetables. (Basil, a heat lover, spoils too quickly when kept in a cold refrigerator.) Passionflowers are laid directly on the table. They easily last an evening out of water, and the one I pinned in my hair stayed so fresh friends thought it was plastic.

*decor*

## SERVING URNS

Right before the guests arrive, two large urns placed on either side of the entrance are filled with ice and sangría, soft drinks, beer, and wine. They have false bottoms, with tin washbuckets inside, making them easier to fill quickly. Guests serve themselves drinks before strolling into the garden. Carafes of sangría are also placed around the garden for refills.

ABOVE: Sangría is conveniently placed for the guests to help themselves.
OPPOSITE: Purple and white lady's-slipper orchids combined with the green and purple foliage of calathea leaves, sprays of green grass, and silvery Spanish moss.

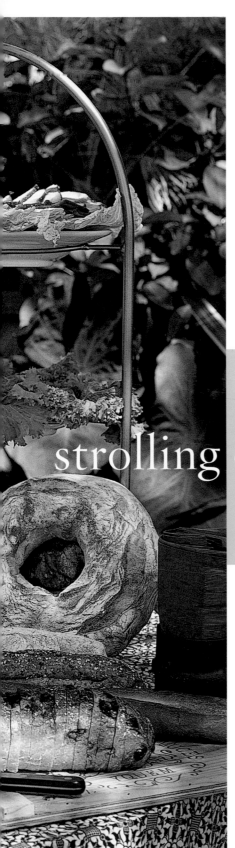

*Sparkling White Sangría*

*Crudités with Assorted Dips*

*Sugared Sweet Potato Rounds
with Crème Frâiche*

*Confetti Shrimp*

*Orange and Molasses Glazed Ham
with Tricolor Roasted Pepper Sauce*

*Spicy Black Bean Spread*

*Roasted Tenderloin of Beef
with Horseradish Cream Sauce*

*Fresh Fruit with Sabayon*

*Chocolate Bits*

MENU FOR 40

# strolling cocktail party buffet

IF YOU'RE SERVING ONLY hors d'oeuvres and the invitation is for a limited time, plan on nine to twelve appetizer pieces per person and skip the dessert. For a cocktail-party buffet with fewer guests, eliminate items from each table but keep the mix.

This is a cocktail buffet, so the food should not only be attractive and delicious, it should be easy to eat. There's enough food and variety that it can be a full meal, one bite at a time; for some people this is dinner; others stop by and then head off to other engagements.

Finger food simplifies everything: Guests may stroll freely without having to juggle glasses,

plates, and cutlery; cleanup is minimized so the morning after isn't spent in a sea of dishes; and a fluctuating number of guests isn't a problem.

Four serving tables are set along the different paths. Closest to the house, a table is laid with the main fare, and guests could immediately see what was for dinner. This is also the place they gathered after a stroll through the garden. Another table near the water-lily pond offers crudités and vegetable chips and one farther out next to a colorful flower border and grass meadow is replete with assorted cheeses and crackers. Dessert is hidden until guests discover the tiki hut, one of several areas where they could sit and relax.

## sparkling white sangría

On a hot summer night, chilled sangría is light, sweet, fruity, and refreshing. When calculating how much you'll need, take into account whether you'll have a full bar or simply a few choices. For forty people, counting on two six-ounce glasses apiece, multiply this recipe by five.

SERVES 8
(TWO 6-OUNCE GLASSES APIECE)

- 1 bottle dry white wine
- 1 tablespoon superfine sugar
- 2 tablespoons Calvados
- 3 tablespoons Cointreau
- 1 teaspoon crème de cassis
- 1 bunch of grapes, stemmed and halved
- 2 pears, 1 peeled and sliced, the other for garnish
- 2 nectarines, 1 peeled and sliced, the other for garnish
- 2 apples, 1 peeled, seeded, and sliced, the other for garnish
- 1½ cups club soda
- 8 strawberries

In a large covered pitcher, mix the wine, sugar, Calvados, Cointreau, and crème de cassis. Add the grapes and sliced pear, nectarine, and apple. Chill in the refrigerator for several hours or overnight. Before serving, pour through a strainer to remove the fruit. Right before serving, add the club soda. Garnish with fresh strawberries and freshly sliced assorted fruit, if desired. Serve over ice.

## crudités with assorted dips

Blanching vegetables is a simple way to capture and hold the fresh flavor of the garden's bounty. Brief boiling heightens their color, preserves their flavor, and retains all their vitamins, while softening their texture. An inch of greens is left on the radishes and carrots as "handles" to hold while taking a bite.

SERVES 40

- 1 pound French green beans (haricots verts)
- 1 head broccoli
- 24 new red potatoes
- 24 baby Yukon gold potatoes
- 24 cherry tomatoes
- 24 radishes, trimmed, leaving 1 inch of green
- 24 baby carrots, peeled and trimmed, leaving 1 inch of green
  - Salt
  - Cucumber-Yogurt Dip (recipe follows)
  - Zucchini Dip (recipe follows)
  - Guacamole (recipe follows)
  - Hummus (recipe follows)

Choose the freshest vegetables, discarding any with spots or discoloration. Rinse and spread on a clean kitchen towel and pat them dry. Chill for up to 2 hours.

Bring 3 large pots of salted water to a boil. Have a large bowl of ice water ready to cool the vegetables the moment they are removed from the boiling water. Add the green beans, broccoli, and both types of potatoes to their own large pots of vigorously boiling water. With a slotted spoon, remove the green beans after 30 seconds and the broccoli after 60 seconds into ice water and allow to chill a few minutes, until cool and crisp. Let the potatoes cook for 20 minutes, or until tender when poked with a fork. Drain and set aside to cool.

When the vegetables are cool to the touch, strain in a colander and spread on paper towels or a dish towel to dry. Refrigerate until ready to serve.

Arrange the blanched green beans and broccoli, the cooked potatoes, and the raw tomatoes, radishes, and carrots on a large platter, accompanied by dipping sauces.

# cucumber-yogurt dip

Cucumber is one of the most refreshing and cooling flavors of summer. This dip can be served with chicken, fish, or raw vegetables. If made with whole slices of cucumber, it can even be served as a side dish or a salad.

MAKES 2 GENEROUS CUPS

- 1 cup sour cream
- 1 cup plain yogurt
- 1 teaspoon fresh lemon juice (from about ¼ lemon)
  Dash of Worcestershire sauce
- 1½ cups peeled, grated, and drained seedless cucumber (about 2 large cucumbers)
- 1 tablespoon minced yellow onion
  Salt and freshly ground black pepper to taste

In a medium bowl, mix together the sour cream, yogurt, lemon juice, and Worcestershire sauce. Stir in the grated cucumber and minced onion. Season with the salt and pepper. Refrigerate covered until ready to serve.

# zucchini dip

MAKES ABOUT 3 CUPS

- 1 large yellow onion, halved and thinly sliced
- 2 tablespoons unsalted butter
- 2 medium zucchini, quartered and thickly sliced
- 2 cups (one 14-ounce can) chicken broth

In a medium frying pan over medium heat, sauté the onion in the butter for 3 to 5 minutes, until it is translucent. Add the zucchini and chicken broth, bring to a boil, then reduce the heat to low and simmer for 20 minutes, until the zucchini is soft. Pulse 4 or 5 times in a food processor, until the mixture is blended yet still chunky. Serve at room temperature or chilled.

## CHEESE TRAY

Cheese has been described by one admirer as "milk's leap toward immortality." I like to serve a mixture of cheeses to please every palate and perhaps introduce guests to something new. Try a Brie or an herbed Brie, a goat cheese, a blue-veined cheese such as Stilton, and a triple-crème such as Saint-André. Remove the cheeses from the refrigerator at least 1 hour before serving so they can reach room temperature, at which point their flavors and aromas are at their best.

# guacamole

MAKES 3 CUPS

 4 ripe avocados, peeled, pitted, and halved
 4 tablespoons fresh lemon or lime juice
 2 medium garlic cloves, minced
 1 medium tomato, diced
 ½ cup chopped red onion
   (about ½ medium onion)
 10 drops Tabasco sauce, or to taste
   Salt and freshly ground black pepper
   to taste

In a medium nonreactive bowl, combine the avocados with the lemon juice and the garlic, and mash to a chunky consistency with a fork. Reserve 2 tablespoons of the chopped tomato and 1 teaspoon of the red onion, and combine the rest with the avocado mixture. Add the Tabasco, season with salt and pepper, and mix gently. (Place in a storage container with a tight-fitting cover, if not using immediately. Before putting on the lid, press a piece of plastic wrap directly on the guacamole to prevent air from turning the mixture brown. Refrigerate until ready to serve.) Just before serving, top with the reserved tomato and onion.

# hummus

Hummus is wonderful as a dip or in summer sandwiches with sliced tomato, lettuce, and avocado. And it is the most nearly perfect food: It contains no saturated fat and no cholesterol or sugars, and it is high in protein and fiber. On top of that, it's simple to make and tastes great.

MAKES 2 CUPS

 1 19-ounce can chick peas, drained
 ½ cup tahini
 2 tablespoons fresh lemon juice
   (from about ½ lemon)
 2 garlic cloves, crushed
 1½ teaspoons cumin

Place the chick peas, tahini, lemon juice, garlic, cumin, and ⅓ cup of water in a food processor and blend until smooth. Serve immediately or keep in a covered bowl in the refrigerator.

# sugared sweet potato rounds with crème fraîche

Sweet potatoes are usually shoved to the back of the mental pantry and reserved for Thanksgiving. I recently discovered how nutritious and wonderful they are, and I've been substituting them for white potatoes in many of my favorite recipes — mashed potatoes, shepherd's pie, baked potatoes, and soups.

MAKES ABOUT FORTY-EIGHT ½-INCH ROUNDS

 6 medium sweet potatoes
 ½ cup light brown sugar
   Crème Fraîche (recipe follows)

Preheat the oven to 350°F.

Rinse the potatoes and poke them in several places with a fork. Place them on an ungreased baking sheet and bake until soft but not mushy, approximately 40 minutes. Allow to cool, then remove the skin. Roll each potato in brown sugar, then slice it into ½-inch rounds. Serve at room temperature with Crème Fraîche as a dip or topping.

# crème fraîche

Crème Fraîche is a slightly tart, raw cream, richer than sour cream, served with fresh fruit and chocolate desserts. It's a favorite in France, and in many American cities it can be purchased at supermarkets. But if you can't find it, here's the recipe. Or substitute sour cream. Make Crème Fraîche at least one day ahead.

MAKES 2 CUPS

- 1 cup heavy cream
- 1 cup sour cream

In a small bowl, whisk the heavy cream and sour cream together. Cover with plastic wrap and place in a warm, dark place for 12 hours. Then stir and refrigerate for 24 hours before serving.

# confetti shrimp

This dish could be an entrée or the only hors d'oeuvre for a formal dinner. For a cocktail party it's served with skewers, eliminating dishes and utensils. When the shrimp is pierced, the confetti of colorful peppers clings to it without dripping.

For the best flavor the shrimp is cooked the day before and marinated overnight in the refrigerator. To serve forty, double the recipe.

SERVES 20

- ½ cup olive oil
- 3 pounds large shrimp (about 24 shrimp per pound), shelled and deveined
- 12 minced garlic cloves
- ½ cup minced peeled fresh ginger
- ¼ cup fresh lemon juice (from about 1 lemon)
- 2 tablespoons fresh lime juice (from about 1 lime)
- 1 teaspoon salt
- 2 teaspoons Chinese hot red chili oil or paprika
- 2 12-ounce jars roasted red peppers in oil, drained and minced
- 2 medium yellow bell peppers, stemmed, seeded, and minced
- 2 medium orange bell peppers, stemmed, seeded, and minced
- 1 cup minced scallions

In a large, heavy skillet, heat 2 tablespoons of the olive oil over a medium-high flame. Add the shrimp and cook, turning once, 3 to 5 minutes, until firm and opaque. Remove the shrimp from the pan and set aside in a large bowl. In the same skillet, sauté the garlic and ginger until soft, about 3 minutes. Scrape the garlic and ginger out of the skillet into a small bowl and mix in the remaining 6 tablespoons of olive oil, the lemon and lime juices, the salt, and the chili oil. Pour the mixture over the shrimp, cover tightly, and let sit overnight in the refrigerator.

Before serving, fold in the peppers and scallions. Serve with skewers for cocktails, or over rice for dinner.

ABOVE: Confetti Shrimp. LEFT: Dennis Schrader chats with guests at his party. OPPOSITE: Dessert in the tiki hut.

# orange and molasses glazed ham with tricolor roasted pepper sauce

Our local butcher, Edward Vassallo, provided this simple yet delicious recipe. When calculating baking time, figure on approximately 8 to 10 minutes per pound.

SERVES 40 GENEROUSLY
FOR A BUFFET SUPPER

- 1 cup molasses
- 2 tablespoons Dijon mustard
- 2 cups brown sugar
- ½ cup fresh orange juice
- 12 whole cloves
- 1 10- to 12-pound boneless ham
- 1 batch of Tricolor Roasted Pepper Sauce (recipe follows)

In a small saucepan, mix the molasses, mustard, and brown sugar. Cook over medium-high heat until small bubbles appear around the edges of the pan. Reduce the heat to low and simmer until the glaze has reduced by half, about 10 minutes. Let the mixture cool 20 to 30 minutes, then add the orange juice.

Preheat the oven to 350°F.

Wipe the ham with a damp cloth. Cut diagonal gashes across the top and sides of the ham in diamond shapes and stud the center of each diamond with a clove. Place the ham in a large roasting pan and spread one third of the marinade over it. Bake for approximately 1½ hours, basting every 30 minutes, until a meat thermometer inserted to the thickest point reads 160°F. Serve with the Tricolor Roasted Pepper Sauce.

## tricolor roasted pepper sauce

MAKES 1 CUP

- 2 teaspoons olive oil, plus more for rubbing the peppers
- 1 large red bell pepper
- 1 large orange bell pepper
- 1 large yellow bell pepper
- 1 teaspoon fresh lemon juice (from about ¼ lemon)
- 2 garlic cloves, minced
  Salt and freshly ground black pepper to taste

Preheat the oven to 450°F.

Rub the peppers with olive oil and place them on an ungreased cookie sheet in the middle of the oven. At 10-minute intervals, turn the peppers until they are soft when poked with a fork and slightly charred, about 30 minutes. Remove from the oven and allow to cool. Peel off the skin, remove the tops, and halve each pepper. Discard the seeds. Coarsely chop the peppers and set aside in a medium bowl.

In a small bowl whisk together the lemon juice, the 2 teaspoons of olive oil, and the garlic, and season with salt and pepper. Dress the chopped peppers, then place in a food processor and pulse until the mixture is blended but not completely smooth. Adjust seasonings and serve.

# spicy black bean spread

This vegetarian favorite can be spread on bread or made into a sandwich with cheese, lettuce, and tomatoes. At parties it can be served as a dip for raw vegetables or tortilla chips. It keeps well in a sealed container in the refrigerator and can be made a day or two ahead.

MAKES 1 1/2 CUPS

- 1  15.5-ounce can black beans, drained
- 1  tablespoon sour cream
- 1  teaspoon cumin
- 1  teaspoon fresh lemon juice (from about 1/4 lemon)
- 1  tablespoon chopped fresh cilantro, plus whole sprigs for garnish
- 2  garlic cloves, minced
- 1/4  cup chopped yellow onion (about 1/2 small onion)
- 1/8  teaspoon Tabasco sauce
- 1/2  cup finely shredded Monterey Jack cheese

Set aside 1/4 cup of the black beans for garnish. Place the remaining beans, sour cream, cumin, lemon juice, chopped cilantro, garlic, onion, Tabasco, and cheese in a food processor. Pulse five or six times, until mixed but still chunky. Refrigerate in a covered bowl until ready to use. Before serving, sprinkle with the 1/4 cup of reserved beans and the cilantro sprigs.

# roast tenderloin of beef with horseradish cream sauce

In every crowd, there are those who love nothing so much as tender beef, and a filet mignon is the most tender. It is also the most expensive, but for a celebratory occasion nothing beats it in popularity. Be sure to remove the roast from the oven just before it is done to your liking; all meat continues to cook a little after it is removed from the heat. Because most tenderloins are thinner at the ends, parts of it will be better done than others, giving your guests a choice.

SERVES 40 FOR A COCKTAIL BUFFET

- 1  12-pound tenderloin of beef
  Salt and freshly ground black pepper to taste
- 8  ounces cream cheese, softened
- 1  tablespoon fresh lemon juice (from about 1/2 lemon)
- 1  tablespoon Worcestershire sauce
- 4  tablespoons prepared horseradish
- 1  cup heavy cream

Preheat the oven to 400°F.

Trim any surplus fat and skin from the tenderloin. Place it on a broiler rack and bring to room temperature, approximately 1 hour.

Place the rack in the oven and reduce the temperature to 350°F. Bake uncovered for approximately 18 to 30 minutes, or until a thermometer inserted in the thickest part of the meat reads 120°F. for rare. Remove from the oven and season lightly with salt and freshly ground black pepper. Cover with a tea towel and let it rest for 20 minutes.

Meanwhile, place the cream cheese, lemon juice, Worcestershire, and horseradish in a food processor. Blend until smooth. In a medium bowl, whip the cream until it forms soft peaks, then fold it into the cream-cheese mixture. Refrigerate, covered, until ready to serve.

# fresh fruit with sabayon

*Sabayon,* the French term for *zabaglione,* is a quick and delicious rich custard to spoon over strawberries or as a sauce on a plain sponge or pound cake.

MAKES 3 CUPS

- 6 large egg yolks
- ⅓ cup sugar
- 1 cup sweetish white wine (such as a Riesling or champagne)
- ½ pound Queen Anne cherries, washed
- ½ pound Bing cherries, washed
- 2 mangos, peeled, pitted, and sliced
- 1 quart strawberries, hulled and washed
- 2 pineapples, peeled, cored, and sliced
- 1 large bunch of grapes, washed

In a large bowl, beat the egg yolks and sugar briefly with a whisk. Mix in the white wine. Cook in the top of a double boiler, constantly stirring over—but not touching—boiling water until thick and creamy, approximately 5 to 8 minutes. Allow the sabayon to cool before putting it in a tightly covered container in the refrigerator to chill.

When ready to serve, put the sabayon in a small bowl in the center of a large platter and arrange the fruit around it.

# chocolate bits

This dense and delicious chocolate treat is one of the top-selling desserts at the Page Two Bakery in Oyster Bay, New York. It is somewhere between a chocolate torte and a brownie, so rich you only need a little bit—hence the name.

MAKES 2 DOZEN

- 6 ounces unsweetened chocolate (Ghirardelli or another top brand)
- 1 cup (2 sticks) unsalted butter
- 5 large eggs
- 2½ cups sugar
- 2 teaspoons pure vanilla extract
  Pinch of salt
- 1 cup sifted cake flour

Preheat the oven to 325°F. Grease and flour an 11 × 17-inch baking pan.

Melt the chocolate and butter together in a small, heavy saucepan over low heat, stirring constantly, until the mixture is smooth. Set aside to cool.

In the bowl of an electric mixer, beat the eggs and sugar together at high speed until they are light and fluffy. Stir in the vanilla and cooled chocolate-butter mixture. Add the salt and flour, stirring just until everything is combined.

Turn the batter into the baking pan and bake in the middle of the oven for 20 to 25 minutes, until a toothpick inserted into the center comes out clean and the bars are still moist. Allow to cool thoroughly before slicing.

In the high heat of summer, passionate gardeners take time to enjoy the fruit of their labors, preferably from the vantage point of a comfortable hammock in a cool breeze. It's a great time for gardeners to get together to view one another's masterpieces. My good friend and fellow garden designer Conni Cross regularly hosts events in her yard for designers and growers to exchange ideas and talk shop. And since

## a gardener's early supper

many of the guests start their day at sunrise, an early supper is a welcome treat.

## the garden

CONNI CROSS DESIGNS GARDENS by throwing convention to the wind, choosing instead to follow her heart. In her own garden, she brought the blooms to her doorstep. Berms tumbling with a rich mix of colors, heights, and textures fan out from the house's foundation in different directions to bloom under every window, next to every wall, and between the doors. In summer, flowering vines hang down from the balcony. She never has to say, "You should have been here last week"; something new is always happening.

It's a collector's garden. Conni's nursery, Environmentals, Inc., specializes in new and unusual plants, and her collection of heaths and heathers has introduced more than a few gardeners to the beauty of unusual plants. Dense plant communities are encouraged and often left to self-sow, occasionally fighting it out among themselves. Her garden is a bit of paradise created with artistry, imagination, and charm.

OPPOSITE: A lushly planted berm next to the house is a mix of perennials, groundcovers, shrubs, and annuals; an empty pot adds a sculptural element. ABOVE: A woodland walk leads to one of Conni's many water gardens. BELOW: Despite the sign, the close plantings and rich texture of gardens leave no room for weeds.

CONNI'S SKILL as a garden designer naturally spills over to entertaining. When she decorates the table, the garden is her creative muse: The centerpiece resembles a miniature garden with undulating borders and dollhouse furniture. A copper watering can that holds a few stems of blue lace cap and oak-leaf hydrangea decorates the buffet table. Nearby, a stone rabbit sits up begging, a wreath of 'Golden Heart' ivy and cherry tomatoes whimsically hung around its neck. (The wreath was made on a floral foam ring that was sliced open on one side in order to slip it around the rabbit's neck.)

## MINIATURE GARDEN

"Designing a dish garden in a long wooden planter with flower clippings is not much different than designing a perennial border," says Conni. The container, a wooden box, is made by nailing juniper sides to a plywood bottom, then lining it with black plastic and filling it with moist soil. Sand or floral foam will work as well.

Conni cuts flowers and foliage in different lengths, from 2 to 6 inches, including sprigs of blue salvia, phlox, butterfly bush, dwarf spruce, sedum 'Autumn Joy', Japanese maple, assorted pines, creeping thyme, heaths, and heathers. The border undulates down the middle of the container to be viewed easily from every side. First, she pokes the twigs, pine tips, and Japanese maple cuttings into the soil to resemble trees and shrubs. Following good garden design, she adds fine and coarse textures, dark and light greens, with burgundy, silver, and gold foliage. Creative license is part of the fun, and you needn't worry about whether a flower needs sun or shade. Place the flower sprigs close together to create a full, lush look. Substitute moss for grass and dollhouse miniatures for ornaments and garden furniture.

Water well and let it drain before putting it on the table. Kept moist, it should last for several days. For evening, candles can be poked into the dish garden to look like garden torches.

OPPOSITE TOP: A whimsical stone rabbit and a copper watering can decorate the buffet table, while a plant stand holds the tossed salad. OPPOSITE BOTTOM: The entrance to the pool and its garden. ABOVE: A dollhouse wicker chair is the right scale for the miniature garden.

*Iced Tea with Orange Juice
and Pineapple Sage*

*Fresh Sparkling Lemonade*

*Green Goddess Zucchini Soup*

*Simply Tomatoes*

*Black Bean and Corn Salad*

*Grilled Salmon*

*Classic Biscuits with Tomatoes*

*Blueberry Tart*

*Mom's Peach Pie*

MENU FOR 8

# gardener's early supper

AS THE SUMMER gets hotter, the party food gets simpler. Dinner is prepared ahead and served at room temperature, and salads are perfect fare. The Black Bean and Corn Salad is best made a day or two ahead; it just gets better as it marinates in the dressing. The salmon is grilled in the morning, then refrigerated and served at room temperature. Unfussy seasonal dishes such as sliced tomatoes, zucchini soup, a peach pie, and a blueberry tart make the meal light and delicious.

# iced tea with orange juice and pineapple sage

When making iced tea, use 50 percent more tea than you would use when making hot tea to compensate for the melting ice. For example, use 4 tea bags (or 4 teaspoons of loose tea) to make 4 cups of hot tea, but 6 tea bags (or 6 teaspoons of loose tea) for 4 glasses of iced tea.

I prefer orange juice to lemon in the ice tea. The orange juice sweetens the tea and eliminates the need for sugar.

MAKES 3 QUARTS

- ½ cup English Breakfast tea leaves
- 1 quart fresh orange juice
  (from about 8 juice oranges)
- 2 oranges, sliced
- 6 6-inch sprigs of pineapple sage

Bring a quart of freshly drawn cold water to a rolling boil in a large saucepan. Remove from the heat and immediately add the loose tea to the pot. Stir to immerse the leaves. Allow it to brew for 5 minutes, no more. Strain it into 1 quart of cold water. Refrigerate until ready to use.

Mix the orange juice with the iced tea and serve in ice-filled glasses. Garnish each glass with a slice of orange and a stem of pineapple sage.

NOTE *Cloudiness doesn't affect the taste of tea, only the appearance. To clear it up, simply add a few tablespoons of boiling water.*

# fresh sparkling lemonade

This homemade lemonade is far superior to store-bought mixes. Once you've made it, you'll be hooked.

MAKES 2 QUARTS

- 1½ cups water
- 1 cup sugar
- ¾ cup fresh lemon juice (from 2 to 3 lemons), plus slices for garnish
- ⅓ cup fresh orange juice (from 1 orange)
- ¼ cup fresh lime juice (from 1 lime)
- 1 quart club soda

In a medium saucepan over high heat, bring the water and sugar to a boil. Boil for 1 to 2 minutes, until the sugar is dissolved. Allow to cool, then put in a covered container in the refrigerator.

Fill a pitcher with ice and add the sugar syrup, juices, and club soda. Stir thoroughly, garnish with slices of lemon, and serve.

# green goddess zucchini soup

Zucchini makes a delicious, nutritious, and low-fat soup, with a creamy, velvety texture without the addition of milk or cream. The skin gives the soup a rich green color and the seeds, cooked and blended into a puree, add rich flavor and texture.

SERVES 8

- 1 large yellow onion, coarsely chopped (about 1 cup)
- 2 tablespoons extra-virgin olive oil
- 3 small zucchini, washed, ends removed, cut into 2-inch pieces
- 6 cups chicken broth
  Salt and freshly ground black pepper to taste

In a large soup pot, over low heat, sauté the onion in the oil for 5 minutes, or until soft and translucent. Add the zucchini pieces and chicken broth and bring to a boil over high heat. Reduce the heat to low and simmer for 30 minutes, or until the zucchini is soft when poked with a fork. Puree one third of the soup at a time in a blender or food processor, starting at low speed to prevent the hot soup from flying out. Pour into a tureen, season with salt and pepper, and serve immediately (for a cold treat, refrigerate for several hours; see Note).

NOTE *The soup tends to thicken a bit in the refrigerator. Thin it with chicken broth, water, or milk (even skim).*

OPPOSITE BOTTOM: Conni Cross, wearing her summer hat, takes guests on a tour of the garden.

## HEIRLOOM TOMATOES

If you grow your own tomatoes or are close to a farmstand with heirloom tomatoes, you are the luckiest of cooks. Otherwise consider planting a tomato plant or two in your garden or in a container. They are well worth the effort.

If room were in short supply and I could grow only one tomato, it would be 'Brandywine', an Amish variety from the 1880s that's legendary for its great flavor. But it's not a great beauty—it's actually rather homely, with its reddish pink marbled skin and light, creamy flesh.

'Green Zebra' is a golden green, with a forest-green stripe. The flesh is a yellowish green, great for brightening a salad and providing contrast with the other tomatoes. While it isn't a tomato I would serve alone, its hint of lemon and lime brings out the best in other tomatoes. 'Yellow Bananas' are plum tomatoes used for making sauce as well as eating. 'Beefsteak', often weighing around two pounds, is one of the most popular. The slices are bright red, meaty, and delicious and large enough that one slice completely covers a large hamburger.

'Yellow Pear', an heirloom from the 1800s, is a clear sunny yellow, only 2 inches long, low in acid and very sweet. It is a prolific vine, and once it starts producing tomatoes it is stopped only by frost.

'Sweet 100 Plus'—need I say more? These bright red cherry tomatoes, 3/4 inch around, are sublime.

## simply tomatoes

Embarrassingly simple to make, and beautiful to look at, sliced tomatoes drizzled with balsamic vinegar and sprigs of basil are a great summer treat.

SERVES 8

> 4 large tomatoes or a mix of large and small (about 3 pounds)
> 1/4 cup small basil leaves
> 1/8 cup balsamic vinegar, plus more for serving
> Salt and freshly ground black pepper to taste

Thinly slice the tomatoes and arrange them on a large platter. Evenly distribute the basil over the tomatoes and drizzle a few drops of balsamic vinegar on each tomato. Season with salt and pepper. Set a small pitcher of balsamic vinegar beside the dish for guests to add more to taste.

# black bean and corn salad

Black beans have a hint of mushroom in their flavor that combines well with corn. These small but mighty legumes are rich in iron, and when combined with peppers that are rich in vitamin C, they increase the body's ability to absorb iron; they are also a great source of protein and fiber. The salad is better if it is made the day before and marinates in the refrigerator in its dressing.

SERVES 8

- 4 ears fresh corn, cooked, kernels cut off the cobs
- 1 12-ounce can black beans, drained and rinsed
- 1/4 cup chopped seeded red or orange bell pepper
- 1/4 cup chopped red onion or scallions
- 1/4 cup chopped fresh flat-leaf parsley
- 1 1/2 tablespoons extra-virgin olive oil
- 1 tablespoon balsamic vinegar
  Mâche or Bibb lettuce, for serving (optional)

Put the cooked corn kernels in a medium bowl. Add the black beans, bell pepper, onion, and parsley. In a small bowl whisk together the olive oil and balsamic vinegar and pour over the salad. Arrange the lettuce as a frill around the serving bowl and add the corn and bean salad in the middle.

# grilled salmon

Salmon is best grilled simply. I always cook more than I think we'll eat because it is so good the next day served cold on top of a salad or with lentils (see page 136).

SERVES 8 TO 10

- 1 side of salmon (about 4 pounds), boned
- 2 tablespoons extra-virgin olive oil
- 1 1/2 teaspoons coarse sea salt
- 1/2 lemon

Rinse the salmon and pat it dry. Lay it on a large piece of aluminum foil. Brush on the olive oil and rub on the salt. Move the fish, foil and all, to the grill. Place 4 inches above a medium-hot charcoal fire or a preheated gas grill. Cook undisturbed for approximately 8 to 10 minutes on each side (see Note). Use two spatulas to turn the fish. The fish is done when the flesh is opaque, firm to the touch, and starting to flake. Using two spatulas, one on each end, move the fish to a platter, squeeze lemon over the top, and serve.

NOTE *The rule of thumb for cooking fish is 10 minutes per inch of thickness, regardless of the length and the cooking method. That said, the best results come with regular checking while the fish is cooking. Poking the flesh with the point of a knife to look inside is the only reliable test. It is best to remove the fish from the grill just before it is done as it will continue cooking with its own heat even after it is off the grill.*

# classic biscuits with tomatoes

MAKES 20 TO 24

- 3 cups all-purpose flour
- 2 tablespoons baking powder
- 1½ teaspoons salt
- 1 cup (2 sticks) unsalted butter, cut into small pieces, plus 3 tablespoons for brushing
- 1 cup whole milk
- 3 to 4 small tomatoes, thinly sliced
- 8 1½-inch sprigs of dill

Preheat the oven to 400°F.

In a large mixing bowl, sift together the flour, baking powder, and salt. Add the 1 cup of butter and mix with your fingers or two forks, rubbing the fat together until the mixture resembles coarse meal. Don't overmix.

Make a well in the center and add the milk all at once. Mix it together only until it forms a soft dough. Knead it 6 or 8 times on a lightly floured board, then roll it out to about ½ inch thick. Use a 2-inch round cookie cutter to make biscuits. Gather together any scraps of dough, knead 2 or 3 times to smooth it before rolling it out again, and cut more biscuits.

In a small pan, melt the remaining 3 tablespoons of butter. Brush a light coating of butter on a cookie sheet and arrange the biscuits side by side on it.

Gently press a tomato slice or a sprig of dill into the top of each biscuit and brush with butter. Bake in the oven for 20 to 25 minutes, until golden. They can be baked earlier in the day and reheated at the last minute.

# blueberry tart

This is different from most berry tarts because it has a mix of baked and fresh berries. The best part about this recipe is that no skill with pastry is needed. Even if you have never baked a tart, you will be successful. The pastry is not rolled out, and it easily lifts out of the fluted pan to stand on its own.

SERVES 8

- 1 cup plus 2 tablespoons all-purpose flour
- ⅔ cup plus 2 tablespoons sugar
- ½ cup (1 stick) unsalted butter, cut into small pieces
- 1 tablespoon apple cider vinegar
- 1 teaspoon cinnamon
- 5 cups blueberries
  Vanilla ice cream or whipped cream (optional)

Preheat the oven to 350°F.

Place 1 cup of the flour and 2 tablespoons of the sugar in a food processor and pulse several times to mix. Add the butter and pulse until the mixture forms coarse crumbs. Add the vinegar and pulse until the mixture is thoroughly moistened and holds together. Gather the pastry into a ball and press evenly into a 9-inch fluted tart pan with a removable bottom.

In a medium bowl, whisk together the remaining ⅔ cup sugar, the remaining 2 tablespoons flour, and the cinnamon. Gently mix in 2 cups of the blueberries. Pour the mixture evenly into the unbaked tart shell. Bake for 35 minutes, or until the filling bubbles and the crust is lightly browned. While still hot, cover it completely with the remaining 3 cups of blueberries laid close together.

Let the tart cool to room temperature, then chill to firm before removing from the pan by gently pushing up on the bottom until it is released. The tart can be left on the pan's bottom and placed on a serving platter. Serve with whipped cream or ice cream, if desired.

# mom's peach pie

I believe I have the only mother who travels with her rolling pin and pastry cloth. Her pie crusts are works of art, and she credits her old-fashioned method of rolling out pastry on a dishcloth rubbed with flour and a cloth-covered rolling pin, also sprinkled with flour. The cloth surfaces are more forgiving and make it easier to lift the pastry and move it to the pan.

SERVES 8

- 2 cups plus 3 rounded tablespoons unbleached all-purpose flour
- 2 teaspoons salt
- 1 cup vegetable shortening (Crisco is the preferred brand), chilled
- 4 tablespoons (½ stick) unsalted butter, half chilled, half softened
- 3 tablespoons whole milk
- 6 cups peeled and sliced ripe peaches (about 6 large or 11 medium, totaling 3 pounds)
- ⅞ cup granulated sugar

Sift 2 cups of the flour with 1 teaspoon of the salt in a medium bowl. Dump the shortening and the 2 tablespoons of chilled butter into the flour mixture. Use a pastry blender to cut the shortening into pea-size chunks.

Mix the milk with 3 tablespoons of water in a glass measuring cup. Make a well in the flour mixture and pour a small amount of liquid into it. The amount of liquid you'll need varies with the moisture in the air. Bring the mixture together, tossing lightly. Repeat with more liquid until the dough forms a cohesive ball. Once mixed, wrap and refrigerate for at least 1 hour.

Meanwhile, prepare the filling. Place the sliced peaches in a medium bowl. In a small bowl, whisk together the remaining 3 tablespoons flour, the sugar, and the remaining teaspoon of salt. Pour over the peaches. Add the remaining 2 tablespoons of softened butter and gently mix until the peaches are covered with the sugar-butter mixture. Set aside.

Preheat the oven to 350°F.

Divide the dough in half. Rub flour into a clean pastry cloth, and sprinkle flour on a covered rolling pin. Roll out the dough into a 13-inch circle. Use the rolling pin to roll up the dough and lift it into the pie pan, then press the dough into the sides of the pan and trim the excess. Fill the pie crust with the peach mixture. Roll out the second crust and lay it on top of the peaches. Trim to a half inch beyond the lip of the pan. Lift the edge of the top crust and slightly moisten the edge of the bottom crust with water, then press the edges together. Fold the upper edge under the bottom crust and flute them together. Use cookie cutters to make leaf designs and cut a letter or a peach shape into the top crust to designate the kind of pie and to allow the steam to escape. Finally, fold a 3-inch-wide strip of aluminum foil over the fluted edge of the pie to keep it from getting too brown. (Remove the foil for the last 5 minutes of baking.) Place the pie on a rack in the lower part of the oven but not at the very bottom. Bake for about 40 minutes, or until the crust is light brown and the filling is bubbling. Cool on a wire rack for 2 to 3 hours before slicing.

## PICKING AND CONDITIONING FLOWERS

Many of the flowers you see in florists' shops have been flown in from other parts of the country, as well as from Europe, South America, New Zealand, and even the Far East. These flowers have been "conditioned" to allow them to be boxed and shipped for a day or two out of water. Using simple procedures borrowed from professional florists, home gardeners can prolong the life of flowers in their arrangements.

The time to gather cut flowers is when the sun is low, in the morning or evening. Stems are apt to wilt quickly if cut in midday, when the sun is hot and the plants are losing water. For most flowers, the time for cutting is when the buds are about half open. If buds are in a small cluster, cut some of them in flower but also include unopened buds, which will become healthy blooms later, lengthening the life of the bouquet. But a few flowers—among them zinnias, marigolds, asters, and dahlias—should be picked in full bloom, or they might not open up.

Use a sharp pair of pruning shears to cut flowers. Scissors tend to pinch the stem, inhibiting their water uptake. Cut stems at an angle to create a larger surface that will absorb more water; a cut flower's ability to drink water determines how long it will live. Cut the stems as long as possible without taking too many unopened buds. This allows more flexibility when arranging the flowers and protects the buds, which are tomorrow's flowers. If there are leaves at the bottom of the stem, remove them; leaves left on the stem under water decay and smell unpleasant. If you cut flowers in the garden and don't put them directly into water, recut their stems after you bring them inside and before conditioning them. The bottoms of the stems begin to dry if left out of water for even a few minutes.

After cutting and immersing the flowers up to their necks in warm water, place them in a cool place for four to twelve hours to allow the stems to fill completely with water before arranging them. Flowers "conditioned" in water up to their necks last longer, even when subsequently placed in arrangements with shallow water.

Flower preservatives, available from florists and nurseries, prolong the life of cut flowers. The preservatives contain beneficial chemicals to feed the flowers and inhibit bacteria from growing. Use preservatives in the water when conditioning flowers

and again in the water for soaking the floral foam or the vase they are to be arranged in. These preparations will keep your flowers healthy, blooming, and holding their heads up high. (Although not as thoroughly beneficial as the commercial preservatives, a few drops of liquid household bleach and 1 teaspoon of sugar per quart of water work, too. The bleach prevents fungus from growing without hurting the flowers, and sugar, a quick-energy food, feeds them.)

If it is an especially hot day and your flowers look droopy when you bring them in, there is a quick fix: Immerse the ends of the flower stems a half inch into boiling water for 30 seconds, while keeping their petals out of the rising steam. Then condition them in a cool place as explained above. Even the droopiest will usually be revived by this treatment. Dahlias, poppies, *Euphorbia*, and other flowers that ooze a sticky liquid when cut need to be cauterized to prevent further loss of these vital fluids. Dip the stem ends in boiling water or sear the ends with a match. Mash with a hammer or split the bottom two to three inches of tough, fibrous, or woody stems to help their uptake of water.

After conditioning (six hours in water), flowers will be able to survive several hours or even a day or longer without water. Cornflowers (*Centaurea cyanus*), for example, can last for four days or longer out of water, looking all the while as though they have just been picked.

Our camp in the
Adirondacks is on a private
lake, so the guests, mostly
neighbors, arrive on
foot or by kayak, canoe, or
motorboat. We're all
vacationing, and the hiking,
mountain climbing,
kayaking, and swimming
help us return home
a little leaner. So, here,
calories don't count.

country breakfast in
mother nature's garden

THE ADIRONDACK STATE PARK, six million breathtaking acres of raw beauty, was molded by glaciers more than ten thousand years ago. Now, ancient forests of sugar maples, yellow birch, beech, spruce, and balsam fir surround the lakes and clothe the mountainsides. Within this park there are areas set aside for small cities and private property.

Our camp is a place for us to enjoy living close to nature. The woods march right up to the shore, where rustic benches and a stone pit for cookouts and campfires wait on the narrow sandy beach. The cabins are set a dozen yards back, where the air is sweet with the perfume of balsam. A rustic gazebo made of branches is the perfect spot for a country breakfast. Splashes of sunlight filter through the trees to the forest floor like ripples on golden ponds. Animals are more plentiful than people: red squirrels, snowshoe rabbits, otter, beaver, deer, red fox, black bear, and moose all inhabit the woods.

I don't tend a garden here. I prefer to tread lightly on the natural setting, adding only a touch of red flowers, million bells, petunias, and fuchsia for the pleasure of the hummingbirds. Years ago when a hummingbird dived at my red toenails looking for a drink of nectar, I knew it was desperate. Ever since, I have hung baskets of red flowers in the gazebo and on the porches.

ABOVE: Gathering woodland treasures for the table's centerpiece. OPPOSITE TOP: The early-morning view of mist rising from the lake. OPPOSITE BOTTOM LEFT AND RIGHT: The Kylloe family—Michele, Lindsay, and Ralph—enjoy coffee and muffins on the dock; the view from the dock back to camp.

decor

THE ADIRONDACK STYLE of rustic arbors and garden furniture created from branches is influenced by nature. What might look strange and even grotesque in a formal setting is right at home in a forest. Instead of trying to disguise the burls, gnarls, and twists of the wood, attention is drawn to the warts and bumps and wrinkles of age. The more extreme or distorted the wood, the more unique the architecture. The natural materials are unaltered and are celebrated for themselves.

Our rustic gazebo was made from dead trees and the fallen branches of golden birch, wisteria vines, and pine. Birdhouses and nests and even a dormant wasp nest snugly fit into the back of a chair or hang from the roof.

Here nature's subtleties shine; the muted brown colors and texture of bark and the many shades of green foliage dominate. We use what we have on hand. A dead tree stump is topped with a round of wood from a fallen tree and turned into a table, where we serve fruit drinks and coffee. A small

## A CAUTIONARY NOTE

"Estimates vary, but experts agree that a minimum of 5,000 different kinds of mushrooms occur in North America. Most of them are bitter or flavorless. A few, however, are choice edibles, and a somewhat larger number are deemed suitable table fare, depending upon one's taste. A handful of toxic species cause some degree of gastrointestinal upset or psychotropic disturbance; a few are harmless on their own but poisonous when consumed with alcohol. And a few notorious species are fatal if eaten. Although experienced mycologists do often eat the mushrooms they find in the wild, such a practice is not recommended for novices." *National Audubon Society Pocket Guide, Familiar Mushrooms* (Alfred A. Knopf, New York, 1990).

ABOVE: A rustic bridge spans a woodland stream. OPPOSITE BOTTOM: The arrangement of wildflowers from the meadow includes red bee balm, bicolor monk's hood, and goldenrod. OPPOSITE TOP: The beautiful pale blue eggs of the Araucana chickens are purported to be healthier, with less cholesterol.

ABOVE: The table centerpiece is a miniature moss and water lily garden made from woodland finds (see sidebar). OPPOSITE: A hollow stump holds a bucket of water to keep the branches of hobblebush and ferns fresh.

arrangement of wildflowers from the meadow includes red bee balm, bicolor monk's hood, and goldenrod. (Lest you sneeze at the thought, goldenrod is not the culprit of hay fever, as many people think. Its pollen is too heavy and falls to the ground. Ragweed usually grows nearby and is the guilty party.) A hollow stump is fitted with a bucket of water for an arrangement of hobblebush (*Viburnum alnifolium*) flaunting its fall foliage amid the quiet green ferns. The forest floor is as soft as an expensive carpet woven from centuries of fallen leaves, pine needles, and moss, which adds a velvety texture.

We often gather woodland treasures for a table decoration, a practice started when my children were young and we made a game out of it. Sometimes everyone started out on a hike with a list — a red leaf, a hairy moss, a yellow mushroom — and other times we collected what interested us. Anything we didn't know by name we would look up. Mushrooms, assorted mosses, berries, fungi, pinecones, wildflowers, ferns, and water lilies were usually among the mix. We placed a piece of driftwood or a tray in the center of the table and added to it as the vacation went on.

## MINIATURE MOSS AND WATER LILY GARDEN

Arrange mosses, mushrooms, lichen, Dutchman's pipe, and water lilies collected from a morning walk to mimic a moss garden on an oval metal tray. The tray protects the tablecloth and can be refreshed with a daily sprinkle of water. This one includes both red and green peat mosses (*Sphagnum capillaceum* and *Sphagnum girgensohnii*), haircap moss (*Polytrichum juniperinum*), and bristly clubmoss (*Lycopodium annotinum*).

*Adirondack Cappuccino*

*Very Berry Summer Sipper*

*Sugar and Cinnamon Mini Muffins*

*Scrambled Eggs with Cheddar and
Chives and Campfire Bacon*

*Crisp Potato Cakes*

*Sinful Sour Cream Coffee Cake*

*Blueberry Cloud Pancakes*

MENU FOR 8

# country breakfast in the adirondacks

EVEN BEFORE THEY STEP on shore, guests are greeted with a whiff of coffee and bacon. Mugs of cappuccino and mini sugar muffins are passed while the bacon cooks. We crowd to the gazebo, where the choices would make a lumberjack grin: Blueberry Cloud Pancakes, Crisp Potato Cakes, Scrambled Eggs with Cheddar and Chives, and Sinful Sour Cream Coffee Cake. To wash it all down, there's a pitcher of mixed berry juice and at least a gallon of coffee. No one will leave hungry. And before the day is done, everyone will have enjoyed some healthy exercise.

## adirondack cappuccino

Coffee cooked in the great outdoors has a special taste. Some say it's the atmosphere; I say it's the method of brewing that surpasses the flavor of drip-brewed coffee. Whatever it is, it is certainly worth doing even if it's in your own backyard. Foamed milk can easily be made without a cappuccino machine, and it amazes guests to be served cappuccino in a place they least expect it.

The proportion of coffee to water is a matter of preference. The rule of thumb is 2 level teaspoons of coffee to 6 ounces of water. The key to making great camp coffee is to boil only the water, not the coffee. Otherwise you might brew brown gargle, the old cowboy name for coffee that could float a pistol or heal a cut on a saddle horse. Boiling causes the grounds to release tannic acid, which causes a bitter taste. You can return the coffee to the outside of the fire to keep it warm, but don't let it boil. And you'll notice an odd ingredient below: The eggshell (and the small amount of egg white clinging to it) helps to settle the coffee grounds to the bottom of the pot.

MAKES SIXTEEN 6-OUNCE CUPS

- ½ **cup coffee**
- 1 **crushed eggshell**
- 1 **quart milk, whole or skim**
  **Sprinkle of cinnamon (optional)**

Bring a spackleware or camp coffee pot of 12 cups fresh cold water to a rolling boil on the campfire, then remove the pot from the fire. Drop in the coffee and let it steep for 4 to 5 minutes. Add the crushed eggshell to settle the coffee grounds before pouring the coffee.

Meanwhile, heat the milk until small bubbles form around the edge of the pan. Pour the milk into a Froth-a-matic to the indicator line on the side of the glass. Plunge up and down quickly 15 to 20 times, until the volume of the milk doubles or triples. Let it sit for a few seconds.

Pour out the individual mugs of coffee, filling the cups halfway. Spoon or pour the froth on top and sprinkle with cinnamon, if desired. Repeat foaming the milk until each mug of coffee is topped with foamed milk.

## very berry summer sipper

What better way to start the day than with a fruit drink rich in concentrations of nutrients—vitamins A, B, and C and minerals such as phosphorus, potassium, magnesium, and manganese. When fresh berries aren't available, a 12-ounce package of frozen mixed berries can be substituted. With the frozen berries the drink is slushy, thick, and rich, like a milk shake. Add a few ice cubes and it becomes so thick and frosty it makes a refreshing dessert, similar to a sorbet, with a lot less fuss. For a nonalcoholic cocktail, mix it with seltzer, club soda, or sparkling water. With the addition of rum it's a frosted rum punch.

MAKES 6 TO 7 CUPS

- 1 **cup strawberries, hulled and frozen**
- 1 **cup blueberries, frozen**
- 1 **cup raspberries, frozen**
- 1 **large banana, peeled**
- 2 **cups fresh orange juice (from 3 to 4 juice oranges)**

Put all the ingredients into a blender. Start with the lowest speed and move up to the highest until everything is blended smoothly. Serve immediately.

## sugar and cinnamon mini muffins

These are similar in taste and appearance to sugar doughnut holes, without all the work of deep frying.

MAKES 4 DOZEN

- 2 cups sifted all-purpose flour
- 1/3 cup sugar, plus 1 cup for dipping
- 2 teaspoons baking powder
- 1/4 teaspoon freshly grated nutmeg
- 2 eggs, lightly beaten
- 4 tablespoons (1/2 stick) unsalted butter, melted, plus 1/2 cup melted butter for dipping
- 3/4 cup whole milk
- 1 teaspoon ground cinnamon

Preheat the oven to 350°F. Grease the mini muffin pans.

In a medium mixing bowl, whisk together the flour, the 1/3 cup sugar, baking powder, and nutmeg. Stir in the eggs, the 4 tablespoons of melted butter, and milk. Spoon the batter into the greased mini muffin tins. Bake for 15 minutes, or until the muffins are golden brown.

Meanwhile, in a small bowl combine the 1 cup of sugar and the 1 teaspoon of cinnamon and stir until blended.

Remove the muffins from the tins while they are still hot. Insert a fork into the bottom of each muffin and dip it in the 1/2 cup of melted butter and then in the sugar-cinnamon mixture. Allow to cool slightly before serving.

## scrambled eggs with cheddar and chives and campfire bacon

We are lucky enough to have fresh-gathered eggs from a friend who raises Araucana chickens, which are purported to be healthier with less cholesterol. I can't attest to that, but they do have great flavor. Although their shells are a pale blue, inside the cracked eggs look the same as other chicken eggs.

Scrambled eggs have more flavor when they are "wet." Take them off of the stove while they are still runny because they'll continue to cook on their own.

SERVES 8

- 1 pound thick-cut bacon
- 16 large eggs
- 1 1/2 cups Cheddar, shredded
- 1/4 cup fresh chives, chopped
- 3 tablespoons butter

Lay the strips of bacon in a large iron skillet. Fry over a hot campfire, turning several times, until each strip is a rich brown. Drain on several layers of paper towels to remove the excess grease before serving.

Meanwhile, whisk the eggs together in a large bowl. Stir in the cheese and chives. Melt the butter in a large frying pan over medium-high heat. Add the eggs and stir constantly, with a wooden spatula, scraping the bottom and sides of the pan, for 3 to 5 minutes. When the eggs are creamy with small curds yet still wet and shiny, remove from the heat. Immediately scrape out into a serving bowl.

# crisp potato cakes

Crispy potato cakes made with Yukon gold potatoes taste richer. I serve them for breakfast with eggs, as a side for dinner, and occasionally for children's lunches topped with applesauce. For an elegant dinner, they make a delightful first course when served in a larger size and topped with gravlax (salmon cured by the Swedish method), sour cream, and chopped dill. And they are gobbled up as hors d'oeuvres topped with caviar and crème fraîche.

MAKES 24

- 4 large Yukon gold or Idaho potatoes, peeled and coarsely shredded
- 1 medium yellow onion, coarsely shredded
- 1 large egg
- 1 tablespoon all-purpose flour
- ½ teaspoon salt
- ¼ teaspoon freshly ground black pepper
- ¼ cup olive oil for frying

In a large bowl, mix the shredded potatoes and onion with the egg, flour, salt, and pepper.

Preheat an electric griddle to 350°F. or heat a skillet over high heat. When the electric griddle or the skillet is sizzling hot, coat it with a thin layer of olive oil. Drop a large spoonful (the size of a golf ball) of the potato mixture on the hot grill and pat down using a metal spatula. Fry the cakes until golden brown, about 3 minutes on each side. Remove them from the grill and place on paper towels to remove any excess oil. Serve warm.

NOTE *The pancakes can be fried a few hours ahead of time and re-crisped in a single layer on a greased baking sheet just before serving.*

# sinful sour cream coffee cake

This classic recipe only gets better with time.

SERVES 8

- ½ cup unsalted butter, plus 2 tablespoons for melting
- 1½ cups sugar
- 2 large eggs, lightly beaten
- ½ pint sour cream
- 1 teaspoon pure vanilla extract
- 2 cups all-purpose flour
- 1 teaspoon baking powder
- 1 teaspoon baking soda
- ¼ teaspoon salt
- ½ teaspoon cinnamon
- ¾ cup chopped pecans

Preheat the oven to 350°F. Butter an angel-food-cake pan.

In the bowl of an electric mixer, cream the ½ cup of butter with 1 cup of the sugar until they are soft and light. Beat in the eggs, sour cream, and vanilla.

In a medium bowl, sift together the flour, baking powder, baking soda, and salt. Add the sifted ingredients to the butter mixture. Stir until smooth. Pour half of the mixture into the angel-food pan.

In a medium bowl, mix together the remaining ½ cup of sugar, cinnamon, and pecans. Evenly spread two thirds of this mixture on top of the batter in the pan. Cover with the rest of the batter and top with the remaining one third filling. Bake for 45 minutes, until golden brown. Meanwhile, melt the remaining 2 tablespoons of butter in a small saucepan. Pour on top of the cake and serve.

## AN ARRANGEMENT'S UNDERPINNINGS

When you want flowers in a basket, on a wreath, atop a candlestick, or in a garland, there are many flower-arranging tools available to help. Bricks of floral foam are invaluable to cut into different shapes; metal candle cups allow you to surround your candles with a small bouquet; and plastic-bottomed rings filled with floral foam are perfect for making wreaths to hang or place on a table (see page 57).

Cut the floral foam with a sharp knife. It loses its ability to hold water if squeezed or compressed. Soak it thoroughly by floating it in water until it absorbs enough to sink and bubbles stop rising from it. Don't force the floral foam under water, or it may absorb water on all four sides while trapping air in the middle—right where the stems of your flowers will be. Use green florist's tape to secure the wet foam to your container. The best arrangements hide the foam with greens or moss before adding flowers. If you are using only flowers, use them abundantly. After you've finished, turn the arrangement to be sure all the tape and foam is hidden.

# blueberry cloud pancakes

These light and airy pancakes are more like mini breakfast soufflés. When cherries are in season, they are a delicious alternative to blueberries, halved and pitted.

SERVES 8

- 4 large eggs, separated
- 2 cups all-purpose flour
- 2 tablespoons sugar
- 2 teaspoons baking powder
- 1¾ cups milk
- 1 teaspoon pure vanilla extract
- 2 cups fresh blueberries
- 3 tablespoons unsalted butter, melted, plus 2 tablespoons butter for frying
  Maple syrup, warmed

In the bowl of an electric mixer, beat the egg whites until they are firm and stand in stiff peaks. In a medium bowl, sift the flour, sugar, and baking powder together. In another bowl whisk together the egg yolks, milk, and vanilla. Pour this milk mixture into the flour mixture and stir thoroughly. Fold the egg whites into the batter and gently stir in the blueberries.

Heat an electric griddle to 350°F. or a frying pan over medium heat. Test the frying pan to see if it is ready by dropping a few drops of water on it. If the water bounces and sputters, the pan is ready. Lightly coat the cooking surface with butter and place the batter in large tablespoons on the hot pan or griddle. Flip over when the edges are slightly brown, 2 to 3 minutes. Cook until the pancakes are lightly browned and cooked completely through, another 3 minutes. Repeat until all the batter is cooked. Top with the melted butter and serve with warm maple syrup.

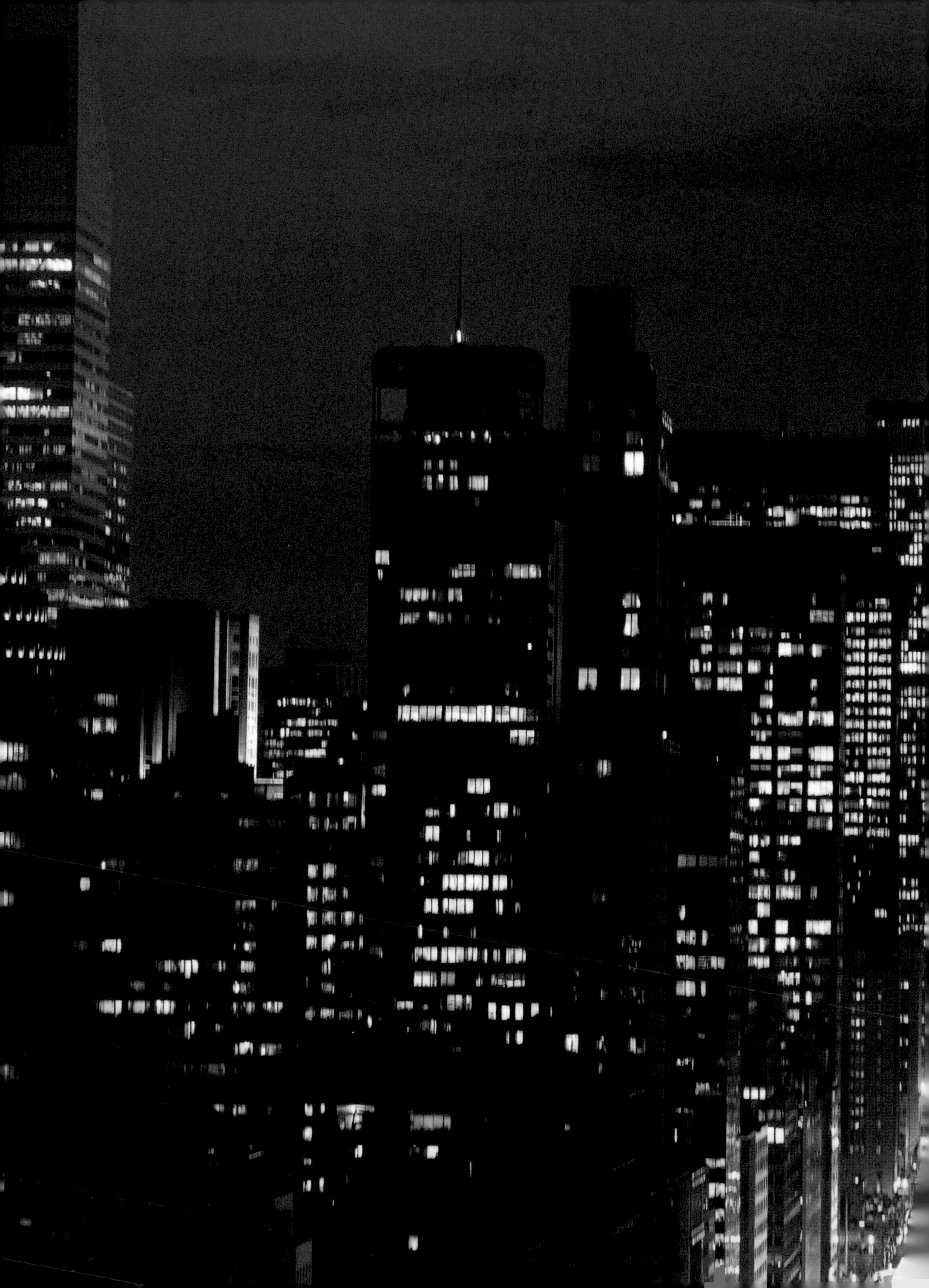

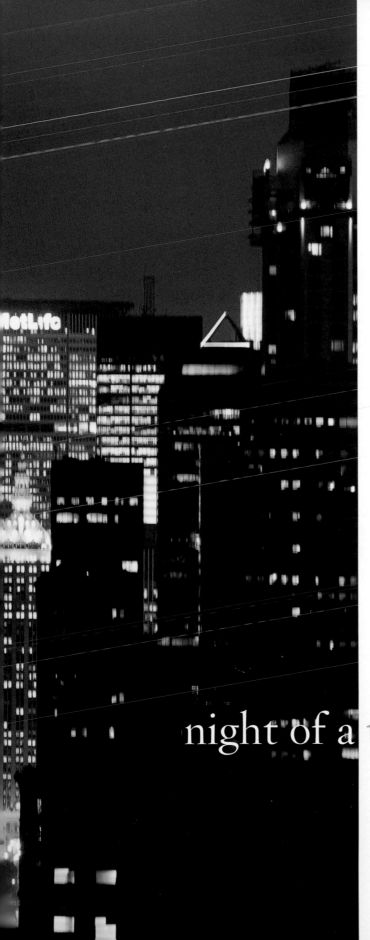

The spectacular sunset is reason enough for a dinner party on Mark and Lorry Newhouse's New York City rooftop garden. The great setting, fabulous food, and interesting guests are the stuff fond memories are made of. Relaxed, impromptu parties like this one with ten friends are held here frequently.

night of a thousand lights

## the garden

MARK AND LORRY'S ROOFTOP combines the serenity of a garden with the grandeur of a magnificent cityscape. Their duplex apartment has wraparound terraces with views on all four sides, and out of almost every window is a garden with a city backdrop. When guests step out of the study onto the open terrace, they are greeted by sweeping views of Central Park, the Hudson River, and the splendor of the city's skyscrapers. At dusk, the city lights brighten and sparkle against the evening sky.

The Newhouses' garden is filled with ornamental cherry trees, crab apple trees, spruces, cedars, junipers, climbing hydrangea, roses, Boston ivy, and a giant seven-foot cactus. Resilient annuals such as double impatiens, million bells, petunias, lantana, morning glories, and geraniums contribute to the colorful mix. The brick walls festooned with vines bloom overhead. The terrace winds around the top of the building, between brick walls and ornate chimneys, and lends itself to setting up garden rooms, each a brilliant, quirky vignette.

ABOVE: A round table is decorated with a metal bust of a woman surrounded by a sea of limes, and an Indian lantern hangs from the awning. OPPOSITE LEFT AND RIGHT: A pot of *Guzmania sp.* adds striking foliage color to the terrace; as darkness settles, the glow of the city lights and lanterns adds sparkle to the party.

ABOVE: The terrace awaits guests. LEFT: A Venetian lantern lights one of the seating areas. OPPOSITE: The garden statue wears a floral wreath.

SIMPLE ARRANGEMENTS of brilliantly colored dahlias and hydrangeas grace the end tables. A pair of silver candlesticks holds an arrangement of greens instead of candles (which would surely blow out in the balmy breezes on the roof). Fitted with candle cups, filled with a scoop of moist floral foam, and secured with florist's tape, the candlesticks hold a harmonious assortment of ivy and evergreens punctuated by red rose hips.

The drinks table is lit up with a huge vase filled with branches from the ornamental cherry and crab apple trees, with hydrangeas, and with some orange dahlias in the fiery hues of the sunset.

decor

## WREATHS

The garden statuary doesn't for a moment rest on its laurels. As an amusing play on history or just for the fun of it, victory has been awarded with a flower mantle. The base of the floral wreath is a small oasis circle first soaked in water and then covered with greenish white hydrangeas, bright orange dahlias, and red rose hips, the fruit of the rose. This same technique can be used on any garden statuary—rabbits, dogs, ducks, pigs, or whatever might strike your fancy.

## IVY-CLOTHED LANTERNS

To dress the lanterns, soak four 2-inch cubes of floral foam in water. Tape one in each corner at the top of the lantern. Place two long strands of variegated ivy so they hang down from the top to the bottom, to soften the edges of the lanterns. Next, poke sprigs of ivy into the floral foam to hide it. Add small orange dahlias and red clusters of 'Scarlet Meiderland' roses as finishing touches.

OPPOSITE: Ornamental cherry and crab apple branches are mixed with hydrangeas and orange dahlias in a vase on the drinks table. ABOVE AND RIGHT: An ivy-covered lantern; Margaret Meacham chats with Doug Hamilton and Donald Portlock.

# night of a thousand lights

THIS FUSION OF DIFFERENT tastes includes an Indian curry, a Greek yogurt, an English pudding, and an Italian bruschetta, which complement one another for a wonderfully interesting meal. Guests help themselves to plates and cutlery, tightly rolled up in napkins on the end table, before dishing up food from the oversized coffee table, whose centerpiece is an antique silver samovar surrounded by colorful condiments.

# bloody mary

The fresh-squeezed tomato juice is what sets this recipe apart. Juice the tomatoes in an electric or manual citrus juicer.

SERVES 10

- 1 46-ounce bottle V-8 juice
- 3 tablespoons Worcestershire sauce
- ½ teaspoon fresh lime juice (from ¼ lime), plus 1 wedge for salting rims
- 1 teaspoon fresh lemon juice (from ¼ lemon)
- ¼ teaspoon Tabasco sauce
- ¼ teaspoon kosher salt, plus 3 tablespoons for salting rims
- ½ teaspoon cracked black pepper
- ¼ teaspoon onion powder
- ¼ teaspoon garlic powder
- 1 teaspoon celery seed
- 2 cups fresh tomato juice (from 4 to 5 large garden-ripe tomatoes), plus thin tomato slices for garnish
- 1 tablespoon prepared horseradish
  Vodka, gin, or tequila (optional)
  Rainbow Swiss chard or a long celery stalk, for garnish (optional)

In a large pitcher, combine the V-8, Worcestershire, lime juice, lemon juice, Tabasco, ¼ teaspoon salt, black pepper, onion powder, garlic powder, celery seed, fresh tomato juice, and horseradish. Mix with a large spoon. Add the slices of tomato, cover, and put in the refrigerator to cool until ready to serve.

Before serving, salt the rims of the glasses: Run a lime wedge around each rim, then dip the glass onto a small plate filled with the 3 tablespoons of kosher salt. The lime quickly dries the salt to the glass.

Fill the glasses with ice. Pour the juice mixture into each salted glass. Combine 3 parts of the juice with 1 part vodka, gin, or tequila, if using. Garnish with rainbow Swiss chard or a long celery stalk.

NOTE *Taste the mix as you prepare it. While most people enjoy the savory blend of herbs and spices, not everyone has a tolerance for spice.*

# tomato-basil bruschetta

*Bruschetta* is the Italian word for "roasted over coals," referring to the grilling of country bread rubbed with garlic and brushed with olive oil. Chopped fresh tomatoes and basil are a common topping, as are sautéed mushrooms or white beans in olive oil and garlic. When the tomatoes are not fresh from the garden, I marinate them for a few hours. They release more of their juice into the oil, and the bread soaks up more of their flavor.

SERVES 10

- 2 cups diced tomatoes (4 to 5 medium tomatoes)
- 2 tablespoons fresh basil leaves, shredded
- 4 tablespoons extra-virgin olive oil
- 10 slices crusty Italian bread
- 4 large garlic cloves, peeled
  Salt and freshly ground black pepper to taste

Preheat the broiler.

In a medium bowl, mix together the tomatoes, basil, and olive oil. Set aside to marinate for a minimum of 20 minutes.

Lay the bread on an ungreased cookie sheet and place under the broiler for a few minutes, until lightly browned. Turn the bread to the other side and brown it. Rub the garlic cloves across the warm bread; the garlic will visibly melt into the bread. Drizzle or brush each slice with the juice from the tomato mixture to moisten it, then top with the tomato-basil mixture and salt and pepper to taste.

ABOVE: Chicken Curry. RIGHT: An Indian lantern hangs from the terrace awning.

# chicken curry

Chicken curry is a simply delicious dish for a crowd. Since it improves as it sits, it can be made several days ahead, freeing the host and hostess to concentrate on other things.

SERVES 10

### For Stewing

- 4 large whole chicken breasts (6½ pounds), rinsed
- 1 bay leaf
- 5 sprigs of fresh flat-leaf parsley
- 1 onion, halved
- 2 carrots, coarsely chopped
- 2 celery stalks, coarsely chopped
- 2 teaspoons chopped fresh thyme or 1 teaspoon dried

### Curry Sauce

- ½ cup (1 stick) salted butter
- 3 medium onions, chopped
- 6 garlic cloves, chopped
- 2 cups diced celery (about 2 stalks)
- 2 cups diced peeled Granny Smith apples (2 apples)
- ½ cup all-purpose flour
- 1 to 4 tablespoons hot curry powder, depending on taste
- 1 teaspoon dry mustard
- 2 teaspoons salt
- 1 cup light cream
- 4 tablespoons Major Grey's chutney
- 2 cups fresh pineapple or 1 20-ounce can pineapple chunks, strained

- 6 cups basmati rice, cooked according to package directions

### Condiments

- 1 cup coconut, shredded, or toasted coconut chips
- 1 cup diced cucumber (1 cucumber)
- 1 cup lightly salted peanuts
- 1 cup raisins
- 1 cup chopped onion or scallions (1 large onion or 1 bunch scallions)
- 1 cup diced pineapple
- 1 cup diced tomato (2 tomatoes)
- 1 6-ounce jar Major Grey's chutney

Place the chicken in a large, heavy stockpot with the bay leaf, parsley, halved onion, chopped carrots and celery, and thyme. Add enough cold water to cover by 3 inches. Bring to a boil, then reduce the heat to low and simmer 30 to 45 minutes, until the chicken is completely cooked. Remove the chicken breasts from the water and allow them to cool. Strain 4 cups of the chicken broth and set aside; discard the solids and reserve any remaining broth for another use.

In a large skillet over medium heat, melt the butter. Sauté the onions, garlic, celery, and apple until the onions become translucent and begin to sweat, about 8 minutes. In a small bowl, whisk together the flour, curry powder, mustard, and salt. Add the flour mixture to the skillet and cook for 5 minutes. Add the 4 cups reserved chicken broth and simmer for 30 minutes, stirring occasionally. The mixture will thicken as it cooks.

Stir in the cream, chutney, and pineapple and mix thoroughly. Remove the skin and bones from the chicken, cut the meat into cubes, add to the simmering sauce, and heat until warm. This can be served immediately or it can be cooled, covered, and kept in the refrigerator for up to 2 weeks. Serve it over basmati rice and allow the guests to sprinkle on the condiments of their choice.

NOTE *Curry is a spice blend that varies greatly depending on where you buy it, even from one region of India to another. Classic ingredients include turmeric, red pepper, coriander, black pepper, cumin, and mustard seeds. If you purchase curry powder from the market, chances are it will not be very hot or flavorful. The best curry powder comes from specialty or Asian markets. Since the mixtures vary so widely it is impossible to give an exact measure for the amount of curry powder. So start with the smallest amount and taste to see if you want to add more.*

## mango yogurt

The rich flavor of the Greek yogurt makes a refreshing side dish for the curry. While a low-fat yogurt can be substituted, it is inferior in taste. Guests are often surprised at how creamy Greek yogurt is, made from Grade A pasteurized milk, cream, and live active yogurt culture. This dish must marinate overnight for the mango juice to flavor the yogurt; otherwise, it is simply mango in yogurt.

MAKES 8 CUPS

- 3 cups diced ripe mango
  (2 large or 3 medium mangos)
- 6 cups Greek yogurt

In a medium bowl, stir the diced mango into the yogurt until it is evenly distributed. Cover with plastic wrap pressed onto the yogurt to keep air from touching it and refrigerate overnight or for up to 2 days before serving.

## lentils

Lentils are among the oldest food consumed by mankind, dating back at least 4,000 years. They are high in protein and easy to cook, requiring no soaking.

SERVES 10 (ABOUT 6 CUPS)

- 3 tablespoons unsalted butter
- 1 medium onion, chopped
- 4 garlic cloves, chopped
- 2 cups (1 pound) lentils, picked over, rinsed, and drained
- 4 cups chicken broth
  Salt and freshly ground black pepper to taste
- 6 tablespoons minced fresh flat-leaf parsley
- ¼ cup chopped cherry tomatoes, for garnish (optional)

In a large pan, melt the butter over medium heat. Add the onion and garlic and sauté until translucent, 3 to 5 minutes.

Add the lentils and the chicken broth. Bring to a boil, then reduce the heat to low and simmer gently with the lid ajar until they are tender and most of the liquid has been absorbed, 15 to 20 minutes. Season with salt and pepper and toss with the parsley. Place in a serving bowl and top with chopped cherry tomatoes, if desired.

OPPOSITE LEFT AND RIGHT: The hostess, Lorry Newhouse, with her dogs; the view at night. LEFT: Chicken Curry with assorted condiments. In the center of the silver samovar is the curry, and clockwise from the lower right are lentils, mango yogurt, and basmati rice; the condiments and miniature pineapples are set directly on the table. ABOVE: Guests gathered around the food.

# summer pudding with chantilly cream

This English dessert more closely resembles a trifle than a custard. Fresh berries are melded together into a mold and cooked just enough to release their juices, which flood the kitchen with their wonderful fragrance. It can be made in any 1½-quart dish, but it holds a shape better if the bowl has straight sides.

SERVES 8 TO 10

- 3 generous cups (1½ dry pints) strawberries, rinsed, hulled, and sliced, plus 10 whole berries for garnish
- 3 generous cups (18 ounces) raspberries, plus 15 whole berries for garnish
- 1 cup plus 2 tablespoons sugar
- 3 tablespoons fresh lemon juice (from about 1 lemon)
- 1 1-pound loaf of white bread, ends discarded and crusts removed, sliced ¼-inch thick
- 1 cup heavy cream, cold
- ½ teaspoon pure vanilla extract
- 1 tablespoon strained raspberry juice (optional)

In a 2-quart nonreactive pan, combine the strawberries and raspberries with 1 cup of the sugar and the lemon juice. Cook over medium-high heat, stirring thoroughly. When the mixture reaches a boil, with tiny bubbles around the edges, reduce the heat to low and simmer for 5 minutes.

Meanwhile, line the bottom of a 6-cup soufflé dish with slightly overlapping bread slices. Trim the bread to fit snugly, and line the sides of the dish with additional bread.

Divide the berries, juice and all, into three equal portions. Spoon one portion into the prepared dish and cover with another layer of bread. Repeat twice more. Cover with plastic wrap, then cover with a plate that fits just inside the lip of the dish. Set a 2-pound weight on top of the plate and place it in the refrigerator for at least 10 hours or overnight. It can be made up to 2 days ahead but it should be unmolded after 24 hours. Refrigerate covered with aluminum foil.

Meanwhile, in a chilled bowl of an electric mixer, beat the cream and the remaining 2 tablespoons of sugar together on high speed until the cream barely holds its shape; it should be the consistency of a cloud rather than a mountain peak. Stir in the vanilla and, if desired, the raspberry juice.

Serve the pudding cold or at room temperature, with a garnish of the cream and whole berries.

NOTE *The cream can be held in the refrigerator for a few hours if it is put in a fine sieve inside a medium bowl. The cream separates slightly as it sits, and this allows the liquid to fall to the bottom without diluting the cream. The alternative is to under-beat the cream and finish it right before serving.*

*Individual clouds of whipped cream measured by heaping tablespoons can be quickly frozen on an aluminum-foil-lined pan. Once they are firmly frozen, in approximately 2 hours, they can be placed in resealable plastic bags until ready to use. Remove from the freezer and place directly on the dessert. They thaw in less than 10 minutes.*

# luscious lemon bars

Lemon is a refreshing summer flavor that goes with almost any meal, and these easy bars can be made ahead and frozen.

MAKES TWENTY-FOUR 2-INCH SQUARES

- 3 cups all-purpose flour
- ¾ cup confectioners' sugar, plus additional for sprinkling
- 1½ cups (3 sticks) unsalted butter, melted
- 4 large eggs
- 2 cups sugar
- 1 teaspoon double-acting baking powder
- 4 tablespoons fresh lemon juice (from about 2 lemons)
- 4 teaspoons grated lemon zest

Preheat the oven to 350°F.

In a medium bowl, whisk together the flour and confectioners' sugar. Stir in the melted butter. Turn out into an ungreased 9 × 13-inch pan. Using your fingers, press down evenly to form the crust. Bake for 10 to 15 minutes, or until the crust is lightly browned.

Meanwhile, in a medium mixing bowl, lightly beat the eggs with a whisk. Add the sugar, baking powder, lemon juice, and lemon zest. Whisk again. Pour the egg mixture over the warm crust and return to the oven. Bake until the edges are lightly brown and the top is firm, about 25 minutes. Allow to cool before sifting confectioners' sugar over the top. Cut into 2-inch squares for serving.

## FLOWERS AND FOLIAGE OUT OF WATER

Even without water, some flowers and foliage are slow to wilt. Flowers that air-dry, such as daffodils, blue salvia, celosia, cockscomb, and lavender, hold their color and shape indefinitely. Many other flowers easily hold their moisture for a day or two, even ones that will not air-dry. Below is a list of flowers and foliage that look good for a minimum of 24 hours, longer if properly conditioned.

| Banana leaves |
|---|
| Blue salvia |
| Boxwood |
| Celosia |
| Cockscomb |
| Daffodil |
| Dahlia |
| Flowering maple |
| Gardenias |
| Grape leaves |
| Hollyhocks |
| Ivy |
| Japanese painted fern |
| Lamb's ear |
| Larkspur |
| Lilies |
| Lungwort |
| Pachysandra |
| Passionflowers |
| Perennial sweet pea |
| Plantain lily |
| Rosebuds |
| Saint-John's-wort |
| Strawflower |
| Yarrow |

There is no better time to serve a garden meal than when there are plenty of flowers, lettuce, Swiss chard, pumpkins, and tomatoes for guests to take home — in most gardens, early October, when the smoldering colors of fall foliage light up the view. Why go to the trouble of having a vegetable garden if you don't make time to share its produce and beauty with friends? Right before the first frost is the last time

## celebrate the harvest

I plan to entertain outdoors, to say good-bye to garden parties for the year.

ABOVE: The table on the left is set for the adults; the children are seated at their own table, within sight of their parents and the garden nanny—a scarecrow in farmer's garb. OPPOSITE LEFT: The wheelbarrow holds the lunch and guests help themselves. OPPOSITE RIGHT: An assortment of fancy gourds, squash, and pumpkins for the guests to take home.

FROM A FEW PACKAGES of seeds planted in the spring, the vegetable and herb garden (with of course some flowers) is transformed into abundant, colorful produce by fall. Some plants—Swiss chard, cherry tomatoes, sunflowers, and zinnia—stay put through the winter. I just can't pick it all.

The corn is finished, a few tomatoes linger. The basil is blooming while the days grow shorter, but on the first cold night it abruptly blackens. Roses, nasturtiums, and dahlias are rejuvenated by the cool nights, standing taller and bursting with blooms. Pineapple sage, a mere seedling a few months ago, is now five feet high, with scented leaves and long red flowers blooming past Thanksgiving. Every year we grow the novelty pumpkin 'Jack-Be-Little', some years up a fence or trellis, other years in a container to conserve space. They are quick to mature, and one vine yields between eight and twelve 3- to 4-inch charming specimens.

Lunch in the garden is a joyous occasion with built-in activities, especially for children to collect seeds, pick flowers, spill drinks, and play among the plants. They are the first to volunteer to pull the red wagon that carts the food from the kitchen to the garden table. If the older guests are game, a pumpkin-carving contest breaks out, and everyone takes home a prized creation.

*decor*

THE COLOR THEME is centered on the hues of the season: fire-engine red, zesty lemon, and ripe pumpkin. Red-checkered tablecloths and informal plates bearing a vegetable motif are appropriate. The bright orange pumpkin 'Ambercup' makes a perfect vase for the fall pick of flowers and berries: black-eyed Susan, pineapple sage, marigolds, dahlias, and bitter-sweet. 'Ambercup' was first hollowed out, then fitted with a plastic bowl liner and moist floral foam. In front of each place setting a nosegay of marigolds, nasturtiums, and love-in-a-puff bobs out of a hollow bell pepper.

Mulled cider is served from a brownish-orange 'Fairytale' pumpkin, so named for its resemblance to Cinderella's coach. Weighing in at fifteen pounds, the large pumpkin makes a good-size punch bowl. It was scooped out and fitted with a glass bowl before it was filled with cider. A squash soup can be poured right into the pumpkin.

## EXTENDING THE LIFE OF ARRANGEMENTS

No matter what type of arrangement you choose, there are a few simple rules that will extend the life of your flowers. Be sure the container is very clean. If you're using commercial preservative, add more warm water to the container daily to replace what is lost through evaporation. If not using preservative, discard the old water and refill with fresh warm water every day to prevent the buildup of fungus and bacteria, which not only smell bad but can stain the inside of the containers. These stains can be difficult to remove conventionally with soap and water. (A tea-leaves-and-vinegar concoction will quickly remove stains. Mix a few tablespoons of loose tea leaves in a cup or more of white vinegar and swish it around inside the stained container until the stain is gone.) Keep the arrangement out of direct sunlight and drafts. You can prepare an arrangement a day or two ahead for a special occasion if you condition the flowers, and store in a cool place (a refrigerator, if you have room, or a basement).

ABOVE: The watering can, so busy all summer, now holds an arrangement of fall fruits and flowers—crab apples, purple hyacinth beans, porcelain vine berries, buddleia branches, Mexican sage, dried Japanese lanterns, and of course ornamental pumpkins.
OPPOSITE: A wreath on the gate, attached by a twist of wire, is wound from the flexible long sprays of bittersweet found growing along the roadside; the orange capsules on the long-lasting wreath gradually open to reveal crimson seeds.

# harvest party

FALL IS THE TIME for comfort food. Orange-Honey Glazed Chicken is an interesting twist on the traditional fried chicken. And even the kids eat these vegetables — Crispy Fried Zucchini, French Carrot Puree, and Double-Baked Potatoes. Apple Cobbler and Toffee-Pecan Bars sweetly finish the meal.

A wheelbarrow serves as an informal buffet table easily pushed into service. The platters of food are set on top of upside-down terra-cotta pots to lift them up for easier serving.

CLOCKWISE FROM TOP: Crispy fried zucchini and mulled cider; the children get a kick out of sitting on giant pumpkin seats—if they can lift them, they are urged to take them home; Justin Swirbul licks the fork clean; Japanese lanterns, hyacinth beans, crabapples, and buddleia.

# mulled cider

Cider is a fall treat, especially when it is mulled and served hot.

SERVES 6 (2 GENEROUS QUARTS)

- 2 quarts apple cider
- ¼ cup orange juice
- 3 tablespoons lemon juice
- ¼ cup sugar
- 6 cloves
- ¼ teaspoon ground ginger
- ¼ teaspoon freshly grated nutmeg
- ⅛ teaspoon allspice
- 3 small and 6 large cinnamon sticks

In a large pot over medium-high heat, warm the cider, orange juice, lemon juice, and sugar until it begins to simmer. Reduce the heat to medium low.

Meanwhile, wrap the cloves, ginger, nutmeg, and allspice in a square of cheesecloth, and tie together tightly with a string. Add the 3 small cinnamon sticks and the spice bundle to the cider mixture. Simmer for 15 more minutes. Serve warm, garnished with the large cinnamon sticks.

# crispy fried zucchini

The big problem with these zucchini is they disappear more quickly than French fries. I usually calculate half a zucchini per person, but it is never enough.

SERVES 6

- 3 small zucchini
- ½ cup milk
- ¾ cup all-purpose flour
- 3 cups olive oil (or enough to cover the bottom of the frying pan with ½ inch of oil)

Rinse the zucchini in cold water. Remove each end, slice in half lengthwise, and scoop out the seeds. Slice each zucchini half into ½-inch-wide strips, and cut each strip into 2-inch-long pieces.

Pour the milk into a small bowl and the flour in another. Dip each piece of zucchini in the milk and then roll it in the flour. Set aside until the oil is hot for frying.

Fill a deep 10-inch frying pan with ½ inch of oil, and heat over high flame until it sizzles. Drop in a quarter of the strips and don't overcrowd the pan. Fry for 2 minutes, or until the strips are golden brown. Remove with a slotted spoon and drain on paper towels. Repeat until all the strips are fried. Serve immediately.

NOTE *While Crispy Fried Zucchini are best straight from the pan to the lips, they can be made a short time ahead if they are slightly undercooked, and then reheated in the oven.*

# orange-honey glazed chicken

Quick and easy to make, this chicken is crispy like fried chicken, yet it is cooked without the skin and baked instead of fried. When children are coming to dinner, I cut one or two chicken breasts into strips to make chicken fingers. They can also be served cubed on skewers for a cocktail party.

SERVES 6 TO 8

- 1 tablespoon vegetable oil
- 5 chicken breasts, skinned, boned, and pounded
- 2 large eggs
- 2 tablespoons whole milk
- 1 cup plain bread crumbs
- ½ cup (1 stick) unsalted butter
- 6 tablespoons fresh orange juice (from about 1 orange)
- ½ cup honey

Preheat the oven to 350°F. and coat two 9 × 13-inch baking pans lightly with the vegetable oil.

Rinse the chicken under cool water and pat dry with paper towels. In a small bowl, whisk together the eggs and milk. Pour the bread crumbs onto a plate. Dip the chicken in the egg mixture, then dredge both sides with the bread crumbs. Make sure the chicken is well coated.

In a small saucepan over medium heat, melt the butter and mix in the orange juice and honey. Cook, stirring occasionally, for 3 minutes, or until the butter is melted and the mixture is smooth. Pour one fourth of the glaze evenly into each of the two pans.

Lay the chicken in the pans without overlapping the breasts, and top with the remaining glaze. Bake for 15 minutes, or until the chicken begins to brown around the edges. Flip and bake for another 15 to 20 minutes, until crispy and golden.

# double-baked potatoes

SERVES 6

- 8 Idaho potatoes (approximately 3 pounds)
- ½ cup (1 stick) unsalted butter, melted
- ¾ cup whole milk
- ½ cup sour cream
  Salt and freshly ground black pepper to taste
- ¼ cup chopped fresh chives

Preheat the oven to 400°F.

Rinse and scrub the potato skins with a brush. Poke several holes in each potato with a fork. Bake for 1 hour, or until tender inside and crisp outside. Remove from the oven, and reduce the heat to 350°F.

Pick up the potatoes one at a time with a pot holder. Cut an oval in the top and scoop out the flesh with a spoon, being careful not to poke a hole in the skin. Put the flesh in the bowl of an electric mixer. Add the butter and milk and beat at medium speed for 1 to 2 minutes, until the potatoes are whipped. Add the sour cream, salt, pepper, and chives and beat for another minute. Stuff the potato shells with this mixture and place in a roasting pan. (The potatoes can be covered and refrigerated for a few hours until 30 minutes before serving.)

Rebake the potatoes at 350°F. for 30 minutes, or until the tops are brown. Serve immediately.

# french carrot puree

Even the children will eat their carrots when they are prepared this way. This recipe from my neighbor Anne Busquet can be made early in the day, refrigerated covered, and reheated in the oven right before serving.

SERVES 6

- **2 pounds carrots, peeled and cut into thirds**
- **1 tablespoon Crème Fraîche (see page 85)**
- **1 teaspoon freshly grated nutmeg**
  **Salt to taste**

Bring a large pot of water to a boil.

Drop the carrots into the boiling water and cook for 15 to 20 minutes, until tender. Drain in a colander.

Puree the carrots in a food processor. Add the crème fraîche, nutmeg, and salt and puree until smooth and blended. Serve immediately.

# quick-and-easy apple cobbler

The light pastry crust is what sets this cobbler apart. It is delicious served hot with a scoop of vanilla ice cream or a drizzle of heavy cream. In the fall, when apples are falling off the trees, I make this quick cobbler often. In the summer, during the short peach and pear season, I use the same recipe to make a peach or pear cobbler. Pears and peaches are juicier, so I leave out the water in the filling.

SERVES 8

**Filling**

- ½ cup sugar
- 2 tablespoons all-purpose flour
- ½ teaspoon cinnamon
- ¼ teaspoon salt
- 1 teaspoon pure vanilla extract
- 5 cups peeled and sliced Granny Smith apples (5 to 6 apples)
- 1 tablespoon unsalted butter, softened

**Batter**

- ½ cup sifted all-purpose flour
- ½ cup sugar
- ½ teaspoon baking powder
- ¼ teaspoon salt
- 2 tablespoons unsalted butter, softened
- 1 extra-large egg, slightly beaten
- ½ pint heavy cream or 1 quart vanilla ice cream (optional)

Preheat the oven to 350°F.

To make the filling: In a medium bowl, stir together the sugar, flour, cinnamon, salt, vanilla, and ¼ cup water. Add the sliced apples and toss until the mixture is evenly distributed. Turn into a pie pan or a 9 × 9 × 1¾-inch baking dish and dot with the butter.

To make the batter: Combine the flour, sugar, baking powder, salt, butter, and egg in a medium mixing bowl. Beat with a wooden spoon until smooth. Using a tablespoon, drop the batter in 7 to 9 portions, evenly spaced, on top of the apples.

Bake for 35 to 40 minutes, or until the apples are tender and the crust is golden brown. Serve warm with a drizzle of heavy cream or a scoop of ice cream.

# toffee-pecan bars

This is a favorite from my childhood. They are similar to a pecan pie, but with a crumb-pastry bottom.

SERVES 6 TO 8 (MAKES 2 DOZEN BARS)

- ½ cup (1 stick) unsalted butter, softened
- 1 cup sifted all-purpose flour, plus 2 tablespoons unsifted
- 2 large eggs
- 1½ cups light brown sugar, firmly packed
- ½ teaspoon baking powder
- ½ teaspoon salt
- 1 teaspoon pure vanilla extract
- 1 cup chopped pecans
- ½ cup shredded coconut

Preheat the oven to 350°F.

Cream the butter in an electric mixer. Gradually mix in the 1 cup of sifted flour. Spread and pat the mixture evenly into a 9 × 12 × 2-inch pan. Bake for 10 to 12 minutes, until lightly browned.

Meanwhile, lightly beat the eggs. Gradually beat in the brown sugar. Add the 2 tablespoons flour, the baking powder, salt, and vanilla extract, and continue mixing until blended. Fold in the pecans and coconut. Spread the filling over the baked crust. Return it to the oven for 25 to 30 minutes, until the filling is firm and the top is lightly browned. Cool, slice into 2-inch bars, and serve.

OPPOSITE: A hollowed-out pumpkin is fitted with a plastic bowl and moist floral foam to hold the arrangement of black-eyed Susans, pineapple sage, marigolds, dahlias, rose hips, and bittersweet.

## ARTFULLY ARRANGING FLOWERS

Flower arrangements need not be elaborate and time-consuming. Float a single fragrant flower (try nasturtium, moonflower, gardenia, dahlia, or dianthus) in a bowl. Put an individual long-stemmed flower (cosmos, lily, salvia, or rose) in a slim, tall vase or cut the stems short and place flowers individually in a series of miniature glass bottles and group them together. Try a tightly packed arrangement of one type of flower in which the flower itself, not the container, catches your eye. Sometimes the flowers are even more effective if the leaves are stripped off and the focus is only on the blooms.

For an arrangement to be successful, it needs balance and harmony of color and form. Color makes the most immediate impact. Group several flowers of the same kind or color together and place another group next to them; continue around the bouquet, adding a slash of blue here, a sweep of silver there. You can get away with adding almost any color if you are careful about which ones touch one another. Stronger, bolder flowers need fewer in their group to make an impact; delicate, softer ones need more.

A mixture of shapes and forms adds interest. Flowers with straight stems give an arrangement backbone. Curving stems add a softness and grace. A lily is assertive and solid, while Queen Anne's lace is fragile and delicate. Play with the juxtaposition of blossoms and notice the contrasts. The stems, often hidden from view, can have a mysterious beauty all their own and may be an integral part of the arrangement if reflected through the water in the vase.

Remember to add interesting foliage. Often colorful foliage by itself is enough to create a centerpiece. The brightly colored, even brassy foliage of coleus looks right at home floating in a Japanese Imari bowl. In the evening, floating candles add sparkle as they reflect in the water.

# acknowledgments

FRIENDS ARE THE MAIN INGREDIENT in this book; without them it never would have been written. First and foremost I want to thank: J. Barry Ferguson, a mentor, an extraordinarily gifted floral designer, and a friend; my father, Ed Frutig, for reviewing the text and making many helpful suggestions; my editor, Christopher Pavone, for his constructive criticism, skillful editing, and belief in this book; and, last but not least, Doug Turshen for designing the book.

Special thanks go to each and every host and hostess: Laurie and John Barry for their beautiful rose garden, Dennis Schrader and Bill Smith for their tropical paradise, Conni Cross for her fanciful garden, and Mark and Lorry Newhouse for their terrace, an oasis in the middle of New York City.

Friends who donated recipes include: Dorothy Frutig, Jane Greenleaf, Mary Ann Jasaitis, Daria Lamb and the Page Two Bakery, Maureen Lodewick, Margaret Meacham, Jayne Mengel, Lorry Newhouse, Gina Norgard, Steven Pregiato, and Edward Vassallo.

Thank you, too, Carter Bales, Shelly Epstein, Lori Hellander, Barbara Isenberg, Sally Kopp, Sue Lehman, Ed and Simone Martin, Carol Schmidlapp, Lydia Usher and Steven Pregiato of J & R Lobster & Seafood of Suffern, New York, and Rothkamp Farm.

Hope and Richard Whitehead drove two hours to bring their daughter, Lorry Newhouse, three buckets full of dahlias and hydrangeas for her terrace party.

José Palacio, over many years, designed and built the rustic gazebo, scarecrow, Adirondack table, and all of the arbors in our garden. Manuel Castillo and Carlos Valle help maintain the gardens.

Thank you to the many photo assistants: Portia Racasi, Michael Calabrese, and Neil Keighlinger.

I'd especially like to thank all of the guests who attended our parties. Without you we wouldn't have had so much fun. You were good sports, everyone.

*Guests at the Sunday Luncheon in the Garden include:* Roger and Sharon Bales, Eileen Pascucci and her two children Nicholas and Carly, and Jane Greenleaf.

*Guests at the Mad Hatter Tea Party include:* Carol Schmidlapp, Rita Hirschfield, Janet Lovett, Beda Lyon, Jane Roll, Mary Beth Donahue, Carol Large, Tracy Vivona, Susan English, Daria Lamb, Christy McNichol, Terry Lindsay, Elise Wallace, Sharon Spivak, and Alecia Mayrock.

*Guests at the Midsummer Night's Dream:* Larry and Carol Schmidlapp, Diane and Raymond Knight, Ruta and Willy Jaget, Carter Bales, Catie Bales, Katie Hirschfield, Jacque and Anne Nordeman, and Michael Ramsay.

*Guests at the Strolling Cocktail Buffet:* Roberta J. Osborne, José M. Zavala, Donna Henvey, Lucy and Garrett Cutler, Roberto Benitez, Robert Simon, Conni Cross, Ann and Bill Pisa-Relli, Joanne Phillips, Jim Glover, Karen and Fred Lee, Marie and Gene Vanden Bosch, Ellen Coster-Isaac, and Maurice Isaac.

*Guests at the Gardener's Early Supper:* Ann and Bill Pisa-Relli, Cindy Wadelton, Dubie Mulligan, Kristin Horne, Bob Simon, Maurice Isaac, Ellen Coster-Isaac, Patricia Coster, Donna Henvey, Skip Wachsberger, Dennis Schrader, Bill Smith, and Frank Clementi.

*Guests at the Country Breakfast in Mother Nature's Garden:* Don and Laurie Meacham, Maureen Lodewick, Keith Desmarais, Gina Norgard, Michael Luppino, J. Barry Ferguson, and Michele, Lindsay, and Ralph Kylloe.

*Guests at the Night of a Thousand Lights:* David Duncan, Shelly Epstein, Doug Hamilton, Steve and Barbara Isenberg, Lana Jokel, Margaret Meacham, Charlotte Newhouse, Donald Portlock, and Betty Sargent.

*Guests at the Celebrate the Harvest party:* Anne Busquet, Andreas von Scheele, Thomas Meacham, Jill Swirbul and her children Justin and Tyler, and Susie Swirbul and her daughters Sarah and Mackenzie Swirbul.

OPPOSITE: Catie Bales and Gina Norgard. ABOVE LEFT: Guests at the Gardener's Early Supper. ABOVE RIGHT: Maureen Lodewick brought her Sinful Sour Cream Coffee Cake to the country breakfast.

# index

# conversion chart
EQUIVALENT IMPERIAL AND METRIC MEASUREMENTS

American cooks use standard containers, the 8-ounce cup and a tablespoon that takes exactly 16 level fillings to fill that cup level. Measuring by cup makes it very difficult to give weight equivalents, as a cup of densely packed butter will weigh considerably more than a cup of flour. The easiest way therefore to deal with cup measurements in recipes is to take the amount by volume rather than by weight. Thus the equation reads: 1 cup = 240 ml = 8 fl. oz., ½ cup = 120 ml = 4 fl. oz. It is possible to buy a set of American cup measures in major stores around the world.

In the States, butter is often measured in sticks. One stick is the equivalent of 8 tablespoons. One tablespoon of butter is therefore the equivalent to ½ ounce/15 grams.

## liquid measures

| FLUID OUNCES | U.S. | IMPERIAL | MILLILITERS |
|---|---|---|---|
| | 1 teaspoon | 1 teaspoon | 5 |
| ¼ | 2 teaspoons | 1 dessertspoon | 10 |
| ½ | 1 tablespoon | 1 tablespoon | 14 |
| 1 | 2 tablespoons | 2 tablespoons | 28 |
| 2 | ¼ cup | 4 tablespoons | 56 |
| 4 | ½ cup | | 110 |
| 5 | | ¼ pint or 1 gill | 140 |
| 6 | ¾ cup | | 170 |
| 8 | 1 cup | | 225 |
| 9 | | | 250, ¼ liter |
| 10 | 1¼ cups | ½ pint | 280 |
| 12 | 1½ cups | | 340 |
| 15 | | ¾ pint | 420 |
| 16 | 2 cups | | 450 |
| 18 | 2¼ cups | | 500, ½ liter |
| 20 | 2½ cups | 1 pint | 560 |
| 24 | 3 cups | | 675 |
| 25 | | 1¼ pints | 700 |
| 27 | 3½ cups | | 750 |
| 30 | 3¾ cups | 1½ pints | 840 |
| 32 | 4 cups or 1 quart | | 900 |
| 35 | | 1¾ pints | 980 |
| 36 | 4½ cups | | 1000, 1 liter |
| 40 | 5 cups | 2 pints or 1 quart | 1120 |

## solid measures

| U.S. AND IMPERIAL MEASURES | | METRIC MEASURES | |
|---|---|---|---|
| OUNCES | POUNDS | GRAMS | KILOS |
| 1 | | 28 | |
| 2 | | 56 | |
| 3½ | | 100 | |
| 4 | ¼ | 112 | |
| 5 | | 140 | |
| 6 | | 168 | |
| 8 | ½ | 225 | |
| 9 | | 250 | ¼ |
| 12 | ¾ | 340 | |
| 16 | 1 | 450 | |
| 18 | | 500 | ½ |
| 20 | 1¼ | 560 | |
| 24 | 1½ | 675 | |
| 27 | | 750 | ¾ |
| 28 | 1¾ | 780 | |
| 32 | 2 | 900 | |
| 36 | 2¼ | 1000 | 1 |
| 40 | 2½ | 1100 | |
| 48 | 3 | 1350 | |
| 54 | | 1500 | 1½ |

## oven temperature equivalents

| FAHRENHEIT | CELSIUS | GAS MARK | DESCRIPTION |
|---|---|---|---|
| 225 | 110 | ¼ | Cool |
| 250 | 130 | ½ | |
| 275 | 140 | 1 | Very Slow |
| 300 | 150 | 2 | |
| 325 | 170 | 3 | Slow |
| 350 | 180 | 4 | Moderate |
| 375 | 190 | 5 | |
| 400 | 200 | 6 | Moderately Hot |
| 425 | 220 | 7 | Fairly Hot |
| 450 | 230 | 8 | Hot |
| 475 | 240 | 9 | Very Hot |
| 500 | 250 | 10 | Extremely Hot |

Any broiling recipes can be used with the grill of the oven, but beware of high-temperature grills.

## equivalents for ingredients

all-purpose flour—plain flour
coarse salt—kitchen salt
cornstarch—cornflour
eggplant—aubergine
half and half—12% fat milk
heavy cream—double cream
light cream—single cream
lima beans—broad beans
scallion—spring onion
unbleached flour—strong, white flour
zest—rind
zucchini—courgettes or marrow